FLIGHTS OF
A NIGHTINGALE

Memoirs of a nurse's wider exploits

By

Judith Ellis

This memoir reflects my recollections of events, locales, and experiences over a period of time. The employment dates, places, and awards named are an accurate record of my life but, in order to maintain anonymity, in some instances I have changed the names of individuals or avoided naming specific places.

For all nursing colleagues and those considering nursing as a profession.

For my three nieces.

So that my memories last forever.

CONTENTS

I wish to thank all my friends for encouraging me to write this book, but in particular Kathy Hale and Frances Binns who helped me to believe that my life may be of interest to others.

PROLOGUE

My childhood made me the confident person who, in 1978, excitedly entered the Nightingale School to train as a Nurse. Expecting to spend my whole career dedicated to working with sick people in hospital, I still feel amazed at how diverse my career has been over the years.

To help readers appreciate the wide opportunities that exist for a Nurse, rather than chronologically describing my own 42-year career, each chapter in Section 2 of this book is a collation of my lifetime experiences in specific areas of practice. The shared stories help to illuminate the ups and downs of my life, illustrating the essential need for resilience and a good sense of humour.

In Section 3, I share how, even with some challenges, I have not only survived but thoroughly enjoyed my life. My memories, even if they personally fade, will hopefully not only interest but inspire others.

PART I

TAKE OFF

Shaped by my family mould,
I started life assured and bold
There was no doubt, right from the start,
To be a nurse was the part
That in my life I was to play
And nothing would stand in my way.

CHAPTER 1

NORTHERN NEST

I was born in a rush on January 1st 1960. My premature arrival took my parents by surprise. No girls' name had been selected and the chosen boys' name, Richard, was thankfully felt to be inappropriate. My sister, Jane, nearly four years older than me, was to be disappointed. On Mum's admission to the maternity unit, she had 'ordered' a boy, or if no boy was available, a dog, a disappointment she seems, 60 years later, to have overcome. Jane had been born in Chester and indeed my whole family were all from the North West of England, but when I was born my father was a lawyer in London and we were living in Middlesex.

When I was two, we all returned to the North West. For my older sister, then six, this was the beginning of playground teasing about her southern accent and a lifelong desire to return south. I, however, although spending most of my working life in London, have always considered myself a northerner.

At 18, partly to assuage my parents' concern that I had chosen to nurse, a career which they believed would leave me forever poor, I made the decision to train at a prestigious London Hospital. I once more crossed that Watford Gap.

Only two of the 100 new nurses starting at the Nightingale School in September 1978 came from 'up North'. Due to my parents' efforts, I did not have a thick Northern accent, but my hard 'a' pronunciation of 'bath' and 'plaque' caused great confusion for the London patients and amusement for my colleagues. I would like to be able to say that, beyond causing hilarity, accents really don't matter but just add interest. However, Mum and Dad were sadly right. I have seen the impact of a broad northern accent in high-level London meetings. Extremely intelligent and innovative northern health professionals have had to work harder to have their input valued, not because of poor content but purely because of their accent.

These days, having spent more years in London than in the North, no one can quite place where I come from, although I do still slip into using northern terms. I have confused many a London cabby by asking them to drop me at a 'ginnel' (def: a narrow passage between buildings); I always refer to going to 'the pictures' rather than the cinema; and have never sorted whether in the evening I am eating tea or dinner.

Being seen as different has, however, had its benefits. On my second day on the wards at St Thomas's, I spontaneously broke the rules by sitting on a bed to comfort, and indeed hug, a distressed patient. The furious and certainly scary staff nurse bore down on me.

"Nurse Ellis get off that bed, IMMEDIATELY," she demanded.

Her tirade was halted by the ward sister.

"Ignore and forgive her – she's from Manchester," she stated with a resigned sigh.

My 'northerness', I am now told by southern friends, is portrayed by my willingness to chat and my approachability. I am not sure that this is about being from the North, but more about the people who influenced me through childhood, my parents and indeed my maternal grandmother, whom I adored. She lived with us and, as both my parents were out working, was my primary carer until she died when I was 11. Throughout my childhood I felt safe, loved, and important. Conversation was encouraged, opinions were listened to and respected, and inappropriate behaviour firmly but fairly corrected. This nurturing environment made me a decisive child, so decisive that I did not hesitate to abscond from activities I disliked.

At four years old my parents enrolled me into ballet lessons on Deansgate Manchester.

My sister loved ballet and I was expected to follow in her footsteps. I hated it. I could see no point in pretending to be a tree or having happy and sad toes! I also knew that, having dropped me off, my parents went for coffee and a chocolate 'club' biscuit in a smart department store restaurant. So, one day, having been dropped off in a pink ballet leotard, skirt, and shoes, I immediately left and followed my parents at a distance down Deansgate, the main shopping street. On spotting me, my parents were probably more scared than cross as this was not a very safe environment for a four-year-old. That was the end of my ballet career, but this was never forgotten by my mother. When I got my MBE in 1998, she announced I should have continued with ballet lessons as I'd stomped across the Buckingham Palace ball room like a farmer's wife.

The second bid for freedom was from my piano lessons at the age of eight. The teacher, Mrs Roberts, was a sweet, elderly lady, but I did not want to learn the piano.

Therefore, one day, having been dropped off at her house, about two miles from home, I told her I would not be coming any more, picked up my books, and left, setting off down the very busy main road. Mrs Roberts, obviously concerned, immediately rang my mother and as I was determinedly walking down the road my mother's car drew up next to me.

"GET INTO THIS CAR!" she shouted through the open passenger window.

"No, I want to think," I responded as I kept walking.

"GET INTO THIS CAR. I WILL DO ALL THE THINKING FOR THIS FAMILY!" was her furious retort. Who could refuse!

My third rebellion was giving the Brownies the sack at the age of nine. The excuse I gave was that they were 'too childish'. The real reason was that as a 'solid' and very weight sensitive child, I was concerned that I would be too heavy for my Brownie colleagues to 'fly me over the toadstool' into the Guides! This resignation would not have been too difficult, apart from the fact that one of my mother's beloved Aunts was Cheshire Commissioner for the Guide movement. On this occasion, efforts were made to bribe my attendance in the form of bronze annual attendance badges. I was not to be persuaded.

I was indeed a strong-minded child and I also had a quick temper. When arguing with my sister I almost immediately recovered, a total opposite to my sister who often remained cross with the irritating younger sibling for some time, long after I could remember what I had done to annoy her.

Generally, I was a contented and lively child at home, but not so happy at the local school. In the infants, I was teased and bullied for wearing an eye patch and little wire glasses, a failed attempt to improve a 'lazy' eye. My dislike of school continued into the juniors, and was reinforced when, due to excessive class size (54 rather than the allowed 50), I was moved up a year. This not only separated me from any friends, but also meant I never learnt my times tables. This was always of great concern to my parents, and of great amusement to my sister, but this knowledge gap has not held me back from effectively managing multi-million-pound budgets in later life!

Missing my friends and being required to repeat lessons that I had already completed the year before, I started my own form of truancy. I used to drag our reluctant dog with me on the walk to school. I'd then tell the teacher that he had followed me, so that I'd have to take him home. On other occasions I told the teacher I'd lost my house keys on the walk in and would need to immediately retrace my steps. I amazingly always returned a couple of hours later having found them. I am sure the teacher was not that gullible, but she never directly challenged me, nor informed my parents.

She did, however, when others were in class studying subjects that I had already covered the year before, encourage me to have library time to complete projects of personal interest. When we cleared my parents' house, we found a selection of childhood illustrated notebooks on such subjects as 'the London plague', 'Snakes of the world' and, of course, 'Florence Nightingale'.

I never knew if my parents were aware of how unhappy I was at junior school, but they were obviously concerned that, although my English was excellent, I was not good enough at maths to pass my eleven plus exam to get a place at a grammar school. They organised a weekly tuition session with a delightful gentleman, Mr Ash.

I enthusiastically attended these weekly after-school sessions shared with the local vet's son. We rotated location, but the most enjoyable evenings were at the vet's house as we were given shop-bought chocolate rolls and orange squash. This was a rare treat coming from a house where we never had squash and only homemade cakes. I've always liked my food, as evidenced by my present-day knowledge of Weight Watchers points and Slimming World Syns.

The tuition may not have helped my long-standing issue with obesity, but it certainly helped me gain a place at Manchester High School for girls, best known for educating the suffragette Pankhursts. I loved it from day one and approached the academic pressure in a very laid-back manner. To begin with I was berated by teachers for not emulating my sister's academic endeavour, but I had my own approach. My mother could never understand why homework, that at the same age had taken my sister all evening, I stated had been completed on the bus journey home.

I was not sporty like my sister. This was a relief to my dad, who had spent many weekends ferrying Jane to netball and hockey fixtures, which the school team never seemed to win. What I enjoyed was helping to teach the younger girls, and participating in the school's charity activity; singing at old folks' homes on Fridays; visiting veterans; helping with children in a local Family Service Unit; etc. I left school with nine good O levels (failed Latin!) and three A levels. My proudest moments were being chosen by my peers to be Deputy Head Girl and being presented with the school's Public Spirit cup.

My childhood prepared me to be interested in all, to respect all, and to feel comfortable and self-confident in any surrounding. I went to a school where, for most families, achievement and position in society were of vital importance. My family kept my feet firmly on the ground. My father was totally disinterested in social positioning, and my mother was as happy eating in the five-star Savoy Hotel in London as having egg and chips at a transport café. I still remember losing her one day when meeting her after a school event and my embarrassment when, in front of my friends' 'posh' families, she appeared, unflustered, from the cleaner's cupboard, and explained she'd gone to check if an upset cleaner was OK.

Our home was an open house to all comers. Elderly relatives were permanently moved in when care was needed; my wayward cousin stayed if he became too difficult for my Aunt to control; Mum's work colleagues appeared and stayed when afraid of thunderstorms; Jane and my friends were always welcomed, etc. etc. It was bedlam and fun, and, looking back, probably stressful for my father. He zoned out each morning with yoga and then just accepted the turmoil around him, until about 10 p.m. when he made it clear visiting time was over by going into the kitchen to noisily riddle ash from the Aga.

My father was a complex individual, an identical twin, but he and my Uncle Jack could not have been more different in character. Jack was an outgoing extravert. He had served in Burma in the war, was a Major in the TA's, on the board of the Manchester YMCA, and in later life secretary of the local Mother's Union! He was fascinated with family history, and indeed proudly traced our family tree back to 1657. He never lost an opportunity to use the family Coat of Arms.

My father had absolutely no interest in genealogy or heraldry and described himself as 'non-clubbable'. He was quiet and kind, with a dry sense of humour, and liked by all. He struggled with depression all his life, and although intermittently on treatment from the age of 17 until his death at 92, his mental illness was never openly discussed. It was only in his later years that Jane and I really appreciated how debilitating this had been for him, and indeed how stressful for my mother. Dad had spent the war as a merchant navy radio operator, which I suppose allowed him to hide away, shunning on board camaraderie.

During these war years he found solace in yoga, which he continued to practice throughout his life. He spent an hour each morning in the locked family bathroom, which was strange, when on holiday, much to my mother's chagrin, he was very happy to shed all when on the nudist beaches!

Dad enjoyed solitary exercise. I have many memories of watching as he swam out to sea, of lugging a canoe down to canals and beaches, and in later years of my mother hiding her embarrassment as he was yet again rescued by the RNLI in Pwllheli when his windsurfer was seen heading out to Barmouth.

Dad's first love, however, was his bike, Walter, which, when purchased, and much to my mother's annoyance, was the most expensive on the market! When my posh school friends drew proud attention to their fathers' shiny new Mercedes, I found great amusement in pointing to my father cycling past us on his blue bike! Walter is still a prized family heirloom, and has regular outings with my eldest niece, Helen.

Dad loved the law but had absolutely no business acumen. He was in partnership with Uncle Jack for many years. This worked for Dad as it allowed him to concentrate on back room, solitary, paper-based, 1:1 activity. His clients loved him as he was thoughtful, thorough, and always kind, including, much to my hardworking mother's annoyance, always charging as little as possible, or indeed waiving charges. Uncle Jack had wanted to be an architect. He was never truly happy in the law practice, but they found a balance with Jack handling anything more outward facing.

My mother was the total opposite to my father, a true extravert. Her father had died of tuberculosis when she was six, and her mother then needed to work. Mum's father was a member of a Masonic lodge so, at nine, she was packed off as a border to the Masonic School in Rickmansworth. She hated it.

She used to painfully describe being sent from Manchester into London during the war years. She crossed paths, at Watford Junction, with children being evacuated North, and nights at school were spent in air raid shelters.

She was teased for her northern accent and was regularly pressurised into performing northern ditties for the amusement of others. 'Albert and the Lion' and 'Miss Nan Knock About' remained family renditions throughout my childhood. School life for her did not improve after the war. Her only happy memories related to morning drill and the friends she made.

Her school years left my mother with a deep need to ingratiate herself and to be liked. She took for granted the close family's affection for her but would fall over backwards to make visitors feel welcome. Jane and I learnt the practicalities of 'family hold back' when meals were served, or not to draw attention to the dryness of our tinned peaches because a visiting child only liked the peach juice!

Although intelligent, due to an illness during her final examination term, Mum left the Masonic school after nine years with no formal qualifications, apart from shorthand and typing. She was, however, a superb ironer, having for years been trusted with ironing the school chapel's altar cloth! She also enjoyed cleaning, and each morning as children, Jane and I would awake to the sound of the vacuum.

Apart from time off when we were very young, Mum went out to work. She was a hard worker, liked people, and I am sure was great fun to work with. Having had various secretarial-based jobs, she eventually became a well-respected school registrar. At 57 she retired to care for my sister's children, to allow Jane to return to work as a doctor, a histopathologist.

Jane and I could not be less alike. Jane has been happily married for over 40 years, and although she enjoyed her work, her family, her husband, three daughters, and now a grandchild, have always come first. I have been fully involved in my nieces' lives, for which I am very grateful as I have had no children. They are my pride and joy. I am described by their friends as 'handy aunty', mainly because of the free long-term accommodation I provided at my London flat, as two of them entered the world of work.

Being an Auntie is a fine balance. You can never expect the closeness of motherhood, but you can always try to be there for them if needed. Sometimes your knowledge of, or involvement in, their life events or plans feels like a bit of an afterthought, but I know that Jane and her family love me and are in their own ways proud of me.

Jane and the girls are extremely close, speak daily, and share everything. They so enjoy each other's company that I sometimes feel a little lonely when in their midst, strangely feeing less isolated when alone in my own space.

I was once told that single people become selfish. I have strived to ensure that this is not true. I do try and consider how any decisions I make may impact on others, including the family, but I recognise that being single has allowed me greater freedom in planning my own life.

As a single and childless person, friendships are incredibly important. I have been blessed with having many close friends throughout my life. My friends, and particularly my many single friends, not my family, are who I regularly chat to about my day-to-day life and to whom I turn in times of stress. Rather than being miserable, or indeed a misery, because I have never had children of my own, I have thoroughly enjoyed any involvement in the lives of my friend's offspring.

As to romance, I am still looking! You could perhaps say that I am too fussy, and in a way that is true. I have had such a great and busy life that the man of my dreams would have had to be quite something to encroach on my life path. There have been times throughout my life when I have questioned why some of the lovely men that I have met have never approached me. Friends tell me I come across as too dependable and independent, and indeed perhaps disinterested in men, which I suppose is true.

This is not because I would prefer a sexual relationship with a woman rather than with a man, but just because my life feels quite complete as it is. I have never had sex, which, if you believe all that you read or see on television, is a rare admission these days. Yes, of course I wonder what I have missed, but I believe sex should be part of a long-term loving relationship. I am honest enough to know this is an easy statement to make when I have never been tempted!

What I do sometimes crave in lonely moments is a relationship with one other human being who is not only interested but totally invested in what I do, to whom my decisions in life really matter as they would have a shared impact. Someone who sees me as the centre of his universe and who in turn I can love and truly share every moment of life with, whether good or bad. My married friends laugh at this vision. They tell me that they envy the freedom I have. They accuse me of seeing marriage through rose-tinted glasses!

Perhaps my idyllic view is because I seem to have been surrounded by couples in successful marriages. I certainly witnessed in my parents' and in my sister's marriage, committed, loving relationships, with family cohesiveness a priority.

My northern childhood was in many ways idyllic. I was loved and respected, protected and guided, but not spoilt, controlled, or molly coddled. I am sure that my parents enjoyed raising their children, but we were not their whole world. That accolade was reserved for each other. I was allowed the freedom to develop as a unique and self-confident individual, a person that my parents clearly loved and cared was happy, but living a life that they never strived to control or indeed fully understand.

My parents died when I was in my 50s, but Jane and her family are still Northern based, and in my retirement I am also now back 'up North'.

CHAPTER 2

FINDING MY WINGS

- General Nurse Training: Qualified (with Hospital honours) Registered General Nurse (RGN) 1981 (Nightingale School, St Thomas's Hospital, London)
- Probation Staff Nurse 1981–1982 (St Thomas's Hospital, London)
- Staff Nurse 1982 (Wythenshawe Hospital, Manchester)

From an early age I was destined to be a nurse. My dolls had many illnesses, and indeed scars. There was no better outing in the 1960s than to the dolls' hospital in Piccadilly Manchester, to get the broken pot head of my china-headed doll replaced. As a young child this was never a rewarding experience as the repaired doll was never quite the same, a Dr-Who-style regeneration. At senior school I much preferred manning the sick room than attending lessons, much to the annoyance of my fee-paying parents.

When I was 11, my beloved grandmother, who had lived with us all my life, was admitted to the first Manchester Hospice. The caring nurses encouraged me to help with mundane tasks, unaware that this was the defining moment for a lifetime career choice. At 16, I returned to the same hospice as a young volunteer. Two evenings a week for two years I watched and absorbed the difference compassionate nurses made to patients as they slipped from this world. My hospice duties began by serving tea and arranging flowers (badly!), but, by the end, I was trusted to sit with patients, sometimes reading to them, or just being there. I commenced my nurse training at 18, appreciating the value of calm compassionate care, focused upon the needs of each individual patient and their close relatives.

Nursing was not a profession my parents would have envisaged or desired for me. They obviously felt duty bound to point out that I would never earn a lot, and would work long and hard hours, with many unpleasant duties. I was more than aware that they would have preferred me to consider law, following in my father's footsteps, or medicine like my sister. This was never directly spoken of, but my bedroom adjoined theirs and I could, through thin walls, hear their night-time discussions. However, I was clear from the start that I wanted to be a nurse, to be there at the bedside delivering care. I was not to be swayed, and they accepted my chosen direction.

Applying for nursing was in itself a challenge. Although all were happy when I considered offers from the three Universities then offering nursing degree programmes, they were less enthusiastic when I rejected these, deciding to apply for hospital-based nurse training. This was not 'normal' for girls from my grammar school, who were all expected to go to University. The school careers room had no information about nursing, but a vast amount of detail on how to apply for medicine.

Eventually, my kindly Biology teacher suggested I send letters to the medical schools and ask them to pass my enquiry letter on to the relevant nurse training school. The decision was made to apply to prestigious London teaching hospitals. This went some way to pacifying my parents that my expensive education had been of value, as these hospitals required those entering nursing to have studied at A level. I was also very aware that I was choosing a challenging path. I did not want to be too near home on those bad days when it would have been all too easy to listen to the 'I told you so' statements and to not persevere.

The first reply was from the Nightingale School at St Thomas's Hospital. My father made it clear that he would take me for the interview, but that I needed to get in as he would not be repeatedly travelling up and down to London. The interview was fascinating. I was 17. We first had a written paper, which I think was to check that our parents had not filled in the forms for us! Then six candidates were put into a room and asked to discuss capital punishment. I was unsure what capital punishment was, thinking it meant being physically chastised at school! Luckily a bright spark opened the discussion with a tirade about hanging as a miscarriage of justice, and I followed her lead!

After an individual interview where, not realising it was the 'Nightingale' School of Nursing, I told the interviewer I had applied there because the hospital had a good view of Big Ben. I was asked to fetch my father to be interviewed! He was unavailable, visiting old haunts from when he'd worked in London. When he did finally turn up, he embarrassed me by announcing that he was not the one wanting to nurse. He proceeded to tell the interviewer how Soho had changed since his day when it had been a good place to source a good night! I doubt my father had ever enjoyed such a night, but he was delighted to shock! I left feeling doomed and got offered an unconditional place the next day!

I commenced my nurse training in September 1978, nervously arriving to meet my new colleagues and three flat mates. My room overlooked Big Ben. Waiting on the bed were my uniforms and the strict home rules. An intercom system in each room, under the control of home sister, ensured no visitors in rooms after 10 o'clock. Our lives were now dictated by the Nightingale School. I loved it.

The academic elements fascinated me. After the drudgery of A level study, it was a joy to be studying things that really interested me and that I felt mattered. Being on the wards was everything I had dreamed of; hard work, challenging in terms of knowledge and skills, but true supportive teamwork, with bad times shared, and so many inspirational role models.

After six weeks introductory training we were released onto the wards, and from that first day I was scared to realise that, once I appeared in my pristine uniform, I was to patients a nurse who could help them. The cry of, 'it's only my first ward' fell on deaf ears. I watched staff nurses glide from patient to patient, always appearing confident and reassuring. I so admired them and hoped one day to emulate them. A lot was expected of us. Standards were exacting. Our Nightingale procedure book became our bible, and indeed even today my bed sheet corners are impressive! Guidance and support were generally there when needed, and not just professional support but a genuine caring approach to our welfare.

The ward sisters, who seemed unforgiving dragons to a scared 18-year-old, ruled the wards, and were all-seeing. On my first Christmas Day, and a long way from home, I found myself in floods of tears whilst nasogastric feeding an unconscious patient. Suddenly the sister appeared, singing 'Silent Night', and much to my surprise gave me a much appreciated and needed hug.

The three years of training consisted of theory and practice blocks and, unlike today's supernumerary students, we were included as an integral part of the workforce. We were left in charge of wards, day and night, from only nine months into training, but senior support was readily to hand. Opportunities to develop our skills and knowledge were never missed, even in the middle of the night, although being asked to state the cranial nerves at three a.m. was a challenge. The sad thing is I can still remember the mnemonic 'On Old Olympus Towering Top A Fin and German Vaulted a Hedge' but not the names of all the nerves!

Ninety-eight women and two men commenced training that September, a sign of the female dominance of general nursing in the 1970s. It was a life-changing experience for most of us; 'nice' girls with very sheltered upbringings who were suddenly thrust into the reality of health care in an inner-city hospital. Every day presented new challenges. My first injection, other than in an orange, I remember well, as it happened to be on the boyfriend of our senior tutor!

My only hiccup during those three years was during a twelve-week placement to the South Western Hospital in Stockwell, London.

Built in 1871 as a smallpox and fever hospital, by the 1970s it was mainly a 'geriatric' hospital. It was a different world from the shining wards that we had become used to at St Thomas's main Westminster Bridge site. In recognition of the unsavoury, and in 1979 potentially hazardous location of the hospital, we were collected and returned from the Nurses home in minibuses, with strict instructions not to miss the transport!

My first two weeks on my allocated 'psychogeriatric' ward was a miserable experience of total drudgery. Each shift was just a constant round of going from patient to patient, cleaning them, feeding them, cleaning them, feeding them, etc., with little help from the dejected permanent staff. It was not only exhausting but soul destroying. Any attempt at engaging with patients was met with derision by the staff. I soon stopped singing the songs I'd learnt for my nursing home concerts when at school.

The horror of this experience came to a head when, on a night shift, I witnessed an auxiliary slapping a patient. I immediately reported this to the nursing officer on duty. She told me to forget what I had seen as that was sometimes how it had to be. I was incensed, and turned to the link tutor for support, only to be told again that it was not up to me to try and change how things were done. An indignant teenager, I immediately wrote my resignation, and self-righteously stormed into the Nightingale Head of School. She listened, and then very calmly ripped up my resignation letter and told me it would be dealt with.

On my very reluctant return to the ward the next day, the offending auxiliary had disappeared. I was so relieved. This experience confirmed for me the importance of tenacity when observing and reporting poor or unsafe practice, not just for the patients' sake but also for your own professional integrity, and indeed peace of mind.

The following week the sister returned, and wow what a transformation. Suddenly every staff member was pulling their weight, so we had more time to engage with and really get to know the patients. Every afternoon she pre-allocated one student nurse to lead on an activity to entertain the patients, and we all rose to the challenge. Nails were painted, concerts held, bingo played, and I will always remember my afternoon of leading Remembrance Day celebrations. It was if a light bulb was switched on in patients who had for that first two weeks been totally uncommunicative. Working for this inspirational sister taught me the impact one person, in the right position, could make.

This was one of many significant and personally challenging events during my exacting training at Thomas's. For some of my fellow student nurses the whole experience of training, or training in London, proved too much. One of my flatmates, who had been struggling with the sadness that comes with nursing dying patients, resigned after nine months, after a particularly traumatic shift. The team had failed to stop a patient exsanguinating from bleeding oesophageal varices.

Another flat mate departed only three days into our training, after four of us were mugged on Albert Embankment, just by the hospital. It was only five in the evening, and the embankment was busy with tourists. Suddenly, I heard the click of a flick knife, a noise I recognised from my Manchester school volunteering days. I turned to see a young man holding the knife to the throat of one of the girls as he demanded we hand over our money. The girl next to me, Anne, who was a law graduate calmly suggested,

"I think our best policy is to scream!'"

We screamed. The muggers released the first girl, threw the fourth member of our group into a wall, knocking her unconscious, and jumped over the wall into the hospital grounds. I turned to passing American tourists to ask for help. They shrugged us away and hurried on.

With no help forthcoming, I turned and ran back towards Westminster Bridge and into the hospital grounds. Collapsing, breathless, across the reception desk, I asked the receptionist to ring the police. Stress is a strange thing. When the receptionist calmly said, "I'll ring Scotland Yard," I hysterically laughed, as I thought Scotland Yard was just a mystical place in books! There followed a surreal evening in a police car trying to spot the muggers, unsurprisingly unsuccessfully! The evening ended with a policeman giving us pots of pepper to throw at muggers if it happened again!

The girl who had been held at knife point, who came from a small Cotswold village, was collected by her parents the next day. I never needed my pepper again, and rejected the hospital's offer of counselling. Going to school in central Manchester had had its advantages.

Nursing certainly made us all rapidly mature and difficult to shock. When I was in my third year, I was confronted by a flasher on my walk home from a night shift on a male genitourinary ward. My immediate disinterested response was, "Put it away. I've seen better all night!'

Nursing in London meant you met all types, and being at Thomas's put us in the centre of London action. In 1981 we cared for those injured in the Brixton riots; we regularly recognised the sound of the air raid sirens which warned of a Thames flood (as this was pre the Thames barrier being opened in 1984); knew how to search and hurriedly draw curtains to limit flying glass when there was a bomb scare; cared for the injured after IRA bombs; and reassured the shocked after the 1979 Westminster bombing that killed Airey Neave.

Our proximity to Westminster meant I cared for several high-profile and senior MPs, who arrived with armed police. These men in blue were eagerly welcomed by the team of young nurses. More than once I was asked to go in an ambulance with a sick MP, to park under the Palace of Westminster to allow the sick MP's vote to be counted if there was a contentious lobby vote.

On one occasion, during Margaret Thatcher's time as Prime Minister, a high-ranking conservative MP was an inpatient, and an enormous blue-based flower arrangement arrived for him from Mrs Thatcher. The MP was discharged two days later and asked us to give the bouquet to any deserving patient. After careful consideration the flowers, with card removed, were placed by the bed of a delighted elderly lady who had no close relatives, and whose left-wing politics were well known to all!

The three years of training can provide many a tale, and each year

I meet up with around ten of the girls I trained with to reminisce about these formative years. The situations we managed, and the traumas we survived at such a young age, have made us close friends for life. I often think these fellow Nightingales understand me better than most.

Having successfully passed final exams, we were all required to work as staff nurses at the hospital for a further six months before being assessed and deemed worthy to receive our coveted Nightingale badges. In April 1982, we all went our various ways. I had my Nightingale wings but now had to fly out into the wider UK NHS.

My training had not prepared me for the reality of hospital healthcare outside a London teaching hospital. I had never worked in an environment where visiting was time restricted and controlled by a handbell, where nursing care plans did not exist and nurses were expected to clear up after doctors, or indeed make their morning coffee.

Nurses were exhibiting the 'hand maiden' approach that I had been taught would have appalled Florence Nightingale! I quietly fought the battle. When a doctor, sitting two paces from the notes trolley, instructed me to stop what I was doing to walk 10 paces to pass him some notes, my response of, "Trouble with your legs, is it?" did not go down well.

Neither did asking doctors to safely dispose of equipment they had used, rather than leaving it by the patient's bed for a nurse to clear.

My first day on a ward in the north I could not believe the panic and subservient obedience of the nurses when a Consultant entered the ward. An extreme example was when I was told to halt all patients eating breakfast, as the consultant found the munching of cornflakes and toast distracting! I refused – I'd never liked cold toast! That consultant never spoke directly to me again, well not until two months later when I had all my long hair cut off and he thought I was a new staff nurse!

At St Thomas's I had been used to mutual respect between nurses and doctors, with the delivery of care on the ward under the auspices of the nurses, with patients' needs taking precedence. I soon realised that, in the wider NHS, I could not take for granted gaining respect from my medical colleagues just because I was proudly wearing my Nightingale badge, or even from delivering consistent high-quality professional care.

I was encountering, and having to grasp, the true societal hierarchical nature of health professions, with doctors at the pinnacle, and nurses struggling to find their place or gain the respect they deserve.

Far from undermining my confidence, this lack of respect, and expectation of subservient obedience that I encountered in those early days as a staff nurse in the North made me even more passionate about my career choice. I had, and indeed still have, no doubt nursing was the right path for me. The self-belief developed from childhood, and the professionalism and pride acquired during my training not only gave me the confidence to progress and constructively challenge but has always guided my actions and frequently protected me from self-doubt.

PART II

PROFESSIONAL FLIGHT PATHS

Nursing provided so much choice
But, guided by that inner voice,
I strived to do what I felt right
And my career really did take flight
Paths followed by heart and head
With ups and downs it must be said.

CHAPTER 3

PAEDIATRIC NURSING

- Child and Adolescent Mental Health Service (CAMHS) Student Nurse Placement 1979
- Nurse at PGL holiday camp 1981
- Children's Nurse Training: Qualified Registered Sick Children's Nurse (RSCN) 1983 (Booth Hall Children's Hospital, Manchester)
- Staff Nurse 1983 (Booth Hall Children's Hospital, Manchester)
- Ward sister – Paediatric Surgery 1983 (Nottingham)
- Ward sister – Paediatric Medicine 1983–1990 (Booth Hall Children's Hospital, Manchester)

Awards/Honours:
1984 – Sydney Hamburger North West England Nurse of the Year Award
1987 – Nursing Standard Child Health Award

In the 1970s, part of general nurse training was an eight-week placement in paediatrics. For reasons I will never know, rather than joining my 98 fellow students on the acute paediatric wards, I was allocated with one other student to spend my eight weeks at St Thomas's Psychiatric Day Hospital for Children and their Families.

This day hospital was located in a two story neo-Georgian house on Black Prince Road, Vauxhall. Although I had volunteered whilst at school to help with 'troubled children' in the Manchester Family Service Unit in Hulme, Manchester – one of the poorest areas of 1970s Manchester – nothing had prepared me for these phenomenal life-changing weeks at Black Prince Road. The house team, all under the leadership of Dr Eva Frommer, comprised of a porter, Fred, a cook, who we called Mrs Bridges (not her real name), a superb sister in charge, Mary Reid, and a variety of other staff, including nursery nurses, primary school teachers, psychologists, therapists, social workers, etc.

The guiding principles of the service, inspired by Rudolf Steiner's understanding of child development, were that to function in the outside world and prevent frustration and depression, young children needed to acquire the skills of understanding and self-expression through the arts. Dr Frommer's controversial treatment model consisted of exposing the children to colour, sound, movement, story-telling, and occasionally prescribing antidepressants.

Each morning started with a staff meeting where we were asked to express through, movement, the colour of the day.

On day one Dr Frommer announced, "Today we are yellow", with arms outstretched, and staff happily moved around the room. To say I felt uncomfortable was an understatement. This embarrassment was increased when all staff were then asked to draw a picture of their day. These pictures were then shared and analysed by the team. I soon learnt to avoid black crayons!

I was, however, meant for this environment. I soon lost all my inhibitions when working with the children. I was happy to act out stories, sing all day, and my morning paintings in the staff meeting became very free flowing, but never artistic! I was delighted when Dr Frommer started taking me with her when she was assessing new patients.

The service was affiliated to the inner-city education authority. The most inspirational excursion I had with Dr Frommer was a visit to a Brixton junior school. They had appealed for help with a totally unruly and disruptive class of eight-year olds. Dr Frommer and I sat at the back of the class. A poor teacher attempted to control the lesson as insults, and indeed missiles, were hurled around. At the end, Dr Frommer sat with the teaching team and, child by child, identified those who she believed just needed stronger discipline and family involvement, and those who had genuine psychiatric issues and required referral.

I loved every moment of my time there, and I still believe the lessons I learnt at Black Prince Road had a greater impact on my practice as a paediatric nurse than any other training that I have done. I remain fascinated by pictures drawn by children, the content and colour revealing so much about how they are coping with illness, treatment, or life. Wherever in the world I have contact with sick children, or indeed when baby-sitting for family and friends, I am known for my continuous singing of nursery rhymes.

In the third year of my training, I chose to spend my final 12 weeks of placement on an acute paediatric ward. My future career plan was becoming clear. I was enthralled by the physical, psychological, and social development of children. I still marvel when observing my great nieces' weekly development. I enjoyed rising to the challenge of assessing a baby or young child who could not tell me what was wrong, 'where it hurt'. I liked working in true partnership with anxious family members, and I thrived on the need for fast analysis, decision making, and intervention in situations where, due to their size, children were likely to rapidly deteriorate.

The final reasons for my decision to enter paediatric were a dislike of slimy dentures and adult feet! Children's feet are cute! I left Thomas's determined to become a paediatric nurse.

I gained a place for a September intake at Booth Hall Children's Hospital in Manchester. Footloose and free from April, I gained a £12-a-month position as a nurse at a holiday camp in Ross on Wye, which provided activity holidays for 90 seven-year olds. What an eye opener! I took with me the Sainsbury book of First Aid and it became my 'bible'!

Nurses are not good at First Aid and I had some scary moments, only survived because my best friend at the camp, Andrea, was an Australian teacher. Her first aid knowledge was superb as it was a requirement for teaching 'down under'.

Andrea was luckily there, and took control, when a member of staff sustained a compound fracture of his tibia and fibula in the middle of the Forest of Dean. The ambulance crews' arrival was delayed for over two hours whilst they argued over whose catchment area he was lying in. Eventually, Andrea made an impressive splint from sticks, which allowed the injured man to be moved to a place where pick up was possible.

I, in comparison, could at first just about cope with the minor injuries: rope burns, insect bites, nettle stings, and splinters – indeed I remain an expert at splinter removal.

Over the summer, with Andrea's calm support, my expertise and confidence as an isolated practitioner fortunately developed as there were many challenging situations. I had, for example, to care for; a child with a fractured skull; a child with third degree burns from being thrown and dragged when a horse bolted after being spooked by a low-flying RAF plane; and even a member of staff's massive oesophageal bleed. The scariest was a three a.m. drive to Gloucester A&E, 60 miles away, with a child having a severe asthma attack. I learnt so much about child health, including that children aged seven actually vomit when home sick. I rarely got a full night's sleep.

I, and the manager, were the only people who slept in the house with the children. All the rest of the staff slept on bakers' crates in a tent village. The staff were mainly under 20 years old. Most evenings they went seven miles to the nearest pub, leaving the manager, me, and Andrea in charge of the children. There were a few sore heads in the morning, and each staff breakfast time we had to tolerate the morning conversations as to which tent zipper had been heard at what time. I had a regular order of pregnancy testing kits at the local Boots! I think the pharmacist thought I was a friendly girl. Nothing could have been further from the truth. I found the whole promiscuous approach unacceptable, and indeed took my responsibilities very seriously.

I think the staff considered me a 'stuck up prude', not helped by the fact that each Sunday I demanded two hours off to go to church, my only escape time. This 'sensible' image did have its advantages. Once the children settled for the evening, and the staff had departed for the pub, Andrea and I had great fun playing a number of innocent tricks on the staff. For example, placing two geese in the tents of inebriated returners, or even turning tents around so that the zip alluded the drunk on their return. We occasionally broke into the tuck shop through a sky light, taking two crunchies and leaving the money and a thank you note on the till. We were never even considered as possible culprits.

At the beginning of September, I was informed that the children's nursing training was delayed until January. My mother firmly informed me that the time had come to get properly paid employment. On a weekend visit home, I wandered into the local Manchester hospital. I was immediately offered a supply staff nurses post, starting on the Monday. I never returned to Ross on Wye but, 40 years on, in spite of geographical distance, Andrea and Martin, her husband, remain my close friends. Most years we holiday together, either in the UK or Australia, and I am delighted that her two sons consider me 'family'.

My children's training went without a hitch. I enjoyed every moment and learnt so much, particularly from one of the play staff, Frances. Frances opened my eyes to the power of play, the vital need to drop all pretentious ideas of professional positioning.

Children do not care if you are senior or junior, doctor or nurse. They want to know that you are honest, caring, and fun. I had to rapidly develop ways of communicating that work with every age group. My time at Black Prince Road, learning about art therapy, was invaluable and it was an advantage that I love singing. My nursery rhyme knowledge rapidly advanced, with 'Miss Polly had a Dolly' still a firm favourite. Frances introduced me to puppetry, and I am still amazed how children will share their deepest concerns with a puppet friend.

To my surprise, my absolute favourite was working with adolescents, a time of such turmoil, and experimentation even when healthy, but particularly challenging if unwell. I discovered that my honest, no-nonsense approach to life seemed to work for these young people. I really enjoyed helping the young people with long-term conditions, and their families, in successfully transitioning from full parental care to independence. It was with great enthusiasm, therefore, that on completion of my children's training, I became a staff nurse on the Professorial Medical Unit at Booth Hall Children's Hospital, Manchester, which tended to take the older children and young people.

I just loved the work but was highly frustrated by the behaviour of some of the senior nursing staff. It came to a head when a very sick adolescent, who I had supervised a student nurse to correctly care for, for five days, collapsed within an hour of handing over to a senior staff member, due to an incorrect syringe drive setting. The patient recovered, but had to be transferred to paediatric intensive care, which terrified her and her family. I was 'instructed' by the senior staff member, who had wrongly changed the setting, not to report the error, and foolishly I obeyed.

A month later a junior doctor, who was leaving, reported the incident. I was summoned by the Director of Nursing for a disciplinary hearing. The chart entries, thankfully, made it blatantly obvious that all was well when I went to lunch and I had not been responsible. For reasons I will never know, the senior nurse was never asked to account for her actions, but trust and respect had been lost, and although I loved the ward, patients, and families, I decided to look elsewhere for a totally different opportunity.

Within a week, I had been offered a junior sister's post on a surgical ward at City Hospital, Nottingham. The ward took regional burns and cleft lip and palate patients. I think I was offered the post because Booth Hall also provided these services at regional level. What they never realised was that I had never worked on those particular wards. I accepted the post, only to be informed as I walked onto the ward on day one that, due to disciplinary and dismissal issues, I was now the Senior Sister.

I was 23 and the ward team comprised of one staff nurse, who started the same day as me, another staff nurse and three mature enrolled nurses (with 10–25 years of service on the ward). They looked nonplussed when I walked in wearing navy. I find myself, even now, surprised that I not only coped, but had a great six months in Nottingham. I cringe when I remember that, on day one, when the 'old timers' announced they all stayed in the ward office to have lunch together, I announced that I was going to the canteen with the new staff nurse.

I added, "Just to let you know that in future no one will be eating in the office, but it's fine for today, as long as you press record on this tape recorder if you're going to discuss me."

I still remember how staggered they looked, and even now feel embarrassed about my youthful bravado in making this demand. I rapidly learnt that they were a great team who had been through a rough time. They were so supportive and loyal, and spared no effort in helping me fill in any gaps in my limited knowledge.

Nottingham City Hospital was at the time considered the poor relation to the brand-new Queens hospital. On frequent occasions I was asked to go and help on the Queens wards. We City folk were easily recognisable as we wore hideous crimplene dresses.

Queens staff were smartly attired in piped cotton uniforms. In addition, I was often late as I always got lost. Following the navigational coloured lines just didn't work for me. I often passed the hospital Tardis at least three times before finding my way.

Living in Nottingham was a delight. My memories include walking in beautiful countryside; ice-skating on the University lake; being disappointed by the limited size of trees in Sherwood Forest (Robin Hood wouldn't have had a chance at alluding capture!); getting very drunk on a colleague's home brew; and learning my first rude Rugby songs in the Ye Olde Trip to Jerusalem pub. I was only 23!

After six months, I received a surprise phone call from Booth Hall from the excellent Senior Sister I had worked for. She sadly told me she had been diagnosed with Multiple Sclerosis and was having to give up work. She asked me to return as the Senior Sister on the medical ward that I had left. I jumped at the chance as I had very quickly realised surgery was not for me. It was too logical and routine. You knew what was wrong with the children and the care they would need. I preferred Paediatric Medicine, where diagnosis was a mystery to be solved, and care, due to rapid condition changes, a constant challenge.

Returning to the ward, I was now in charge of the senior nurse who had triggered my earlier move. However, I soon realised she was fundamentally a kind, caring individual, probably a bit insecure, and perhaps a little lazy. Managing her so early in my career helpfully taught me the value of being really clear about role expectations, the need to be consistent as a manager, to deal with poor performance as it occurs, and the importance of leading by example. A very simple example was that, even if this senior staff member was the only free member of staff, she believed putting linen and stores away was beneath her. She slowly seemed to realise this was not acceptable when she saw that I was very happy to 'muck in' whatever needed to be done.

However, I cannot fool myself, she didn't continue to 'drag her feet' if there was any chance of not helping, particularly when I was not on duty. What had a more sustainable impact was the positive enthusiasm of all the rest of the team, which I think in a way shamed her into action.

Being a manager at such a young age brings many challenges, but particularly when returning to a setting where you have previously had a junior position. One of the most difficult situations was being undermined by one of the auxiliaries. She was a lovely, motherly, but quite opinionated lady, and overly supportive of junior staff.

"Take no notice of Judith, she was a staff nurse not long ago," she could be heard telling staff if I tried to correct their unacceptable practice. When I asked her to desist, she was not pleased. The next thing I knew, her husband, who was a senior police officer, appeared on the ward asking to speak to me. I was very alarmed.

"Judith, a bit of advice for you," he said. "You are the boss now, just tell my wife to 'but out.' What you say goes and if she doesn't like it, she knows what she can do!"

Through advice like this I learnt fast, and I always say that my days as a paediatric ward sister were probably the best days of my career. The ward was my world, and I loved it.

No day was the same. We cared for a wide range of children, from new-born to adolescents, many admitted critically ill, for example suffering from serious respiratory conditions or meningitis, and others with long-term conditions. The ward specialised in the care of children with cystic fibrosis and eczema.

With every sick child came the need to care for the whole family, the need to reassure the anxious and distressed. I always felt the honour and incredible weight of responsibility of being trusted by parents as they handed into our arms their beloved children. As the sister, I recognised that I had to appoint, and manage, a team worthy and deserving of that trust, but also a team that were eager to serve.

And what a team we had.

We loved our jobs. Through all the challenges we never lost the fun of working with children.

Over these years I received two awards. The first in 1984 was the Sir Sydney Hamburger Rising Star Award from the NW Regional Health Authority. To be honest, I am still not very sure why I was selected, but what I clearly remember is the formal afternoon tea presentation event. My parents had accompanied me, and there was copious handshaking with the great and the good of the health service. Suddenly, my father, never a great one for such social events, unexpectedly tipped his plate and, as if in slow motion, we all froze as his cream scone slipped, cream side down, onto the Chair of the Regional Health Authorities brown suede shoe!

"Mine I believe," my father calmly stated as he scooped it up.

In 1987 my parents, under strict orders to behave, accompanied me to the Dorchester Hotel to receive the Nursing Standard Child Health Award. The event was enjoyed without incident. The greatest accolade for me as a ward sister was, however, that student nurses, who had spent time with us on placement, on qualifying were always eager to return to work as part of the team.

As a team we were given freedom to innovate; for example, introducing new models of care and paperwork and introducing named nurses for our children who faced prolonged or repeated admission. The named nurses got to know their allocated children and their whole families so well that care was truly individualised. We knew, for example, what scared and distracted the patients; what food would tempt; what they liked to do; and what helped make any required treatment acceptable.

We realised the negative impact of a child's hospital admission on the whole family, particularly if the children had to have repeated or regular admissions. The siblings' needs often had to take second place to those of the sick child, and parents just looked exhausted. Many families experienced marital problems, perhaps caused by enforced separation due to one parent being resident on the ward. For the admitted children, not only did their education suffer but, being so inconsistently at home and at school, also meant that they had trouble making and keeping friends.

These concerns led to us deciding to introduce home intravenous therapy for the children with Cystic Fibrosis, who at that time required two-week admission every three months, for a course of IV antibiotics. With the support of the Consultant, we decided to train parents to administer the intravenous drugs at home. In 1982 this was a new innovation, and certainly met with some opposition.

Several of the ward team liked repeatedly caring for the same children, enjoying being family substitutes. District Nurses, who were not paediatrically trained, would not get involved, and GPs were not prepared to prescribe, as the cost of the antibiotics would then be taken from the GP's rather than the hospital's budget. The most distressing incident, which really made us question the change that we had put into motion, was when a father of one child took his own life. He apparently stated in a note that, without regular inpatient contact and reassurance from the health service team, his son's CF diagnosis, and his responsibilities, all felt too much to bear. Although incredibly difficult at the time, when we reviewed all the family circumstance assessments that had been undertaken, and the community support that we had put in place for these families, we had to accept that nothing could have predicted this horrific outcome for this particular family.

There was also a professional challenge to this initiative that was hard to handle. I received a letter from the paediatric lead at the Royal College of Nursing. She expressed her view that I should stop this development as it was putting children at risk. I was initially upset, naively believing everyone would always support developments that were better for patients, on this occasion keeping children at home. I could not believe that, as she suggested, any parent would use the IV cannula access to harm their child. It was my first lesson in managing others' risk-averse attitudes.

Later in my career, I was to come across cases of Fabricated and Induced Illness, when parents did deliberately harm their children. I have, however, remained convinced about the rarity of such situations.

What these early experiences did instil in me, was that to introduce innovative practice needs realistic risk assessment and risk management. I have continued to believe that nurses should not be so risk-averse that developments are avoided.

Ward 4 was a safe but also fun place to work and to be a patient. Nurses and doctors all worked as one dedicated team. The Consultant's office was on the ward and his door was always open if any of the staff needed guidance, and more importantly for the parents and children. The children did not hesitate to wander in, telling the Consultant that, for example, an 'eczema cream stung', or they 'wanted a long line rather than so many cannulas'. He always came down to their level and seriously discussed options so they could agree a plan. This Consultant, many members of the junior medical staff and the ward nursing team, including Frances, the play leader, have remained friends for life, partly as we have shared memories of some great shenanigans.

The staff were so dedicated and never hesitated to give their own time to entertain our young patients, as well as the resident parents and visiting siblings. We all worked together to improve the ward environment, papering walls, painting windows, and displaying children's artwork. My artistic talent is limited, and I was always thrilled to praise others' efforts, until one Monday when a well-meaning staff nurse revealed the stairwell window. It was magnificently painted with Pooh Bear with his flying red balloon. The only problem she had used gloss paint. We spent many hours trying to remove it before the works department noticed.

We celebrated every event we could find, from Halloween to the Grand National, and of course Christmas. The lead up to Christmas Day was great fun and each year we organised a massive Christmas fancy dress party, attended by all long-term patients. A year I remember well was my appearance as Mrs Claus in what I now know was a rather revealing costume for a buxom 24-year-old. It was the only thing still available in the fancy- dress shop when I had rushed in the day before. It seemed to be well accepted by the fathers present! Father Christmas (a friend, Tony, who was far better attired, and padded with two cushions), always attended with presents for all, often provided by Manchester Prison service.

Christmas Day itself was not so good. Ward 4 was the only general medical ward to always stay open due to our long-term patients, and every child that could possibly spend even the day at home was discharged. The patients left on the ward were mainly babies and all were critically ill. They were totally unaware of the importance of the day or that this was their first, and sadly for some their last Christmas Day. Staff tried for the sake of parents and siblings, and indeed for their own welfare, to maintain a semblance of festivity.

Night staff, much to the horror of Boxing Day cleaners, put wellington footprints down the ward with paint and fairy dust (glitter). Whole families were invited to come in and share the food offerings laid out in the playroom. Siblings also received gifts, and we particularly attempted to entertain and cheer them as this situation was certainly not great fun for them.

Carol singers were very welcome visitors and were given sherry in medicine pots, but were banned from singing 'Away in a Manger'. We had learnt the line 'and fit us for heaven to live with thee there,' triggered many tears when sitting with a sick child.

Admissions did not stop because it was Christmas, and it was always a long and exhausting day for all staff. We were relieved to welcome back our normal mixed clientele.

Day by day the ward was a lively fun environment with constant fun activities to distract children from the traumas of a hospital admission. Treasure hunts and obstacle courses were enjoyed, and, on most Sundays, we had custard pie fights. These allowed all involved to let off steam, an event which was eagerly joined by even the most senior doctors. For the older children, being allowed to throw a custard pie in the face of a doctor who had earlier been responsible for inflicting pain by, for example, re-siting a cannula, appeared to not only release tension but removed fear of future essential clinical interactions.

For our repeat admission or long-term patients, coach trips were organised to Blackpool and Alton Towers, and weeklong holidays in Centre Park Nottingham, funded by the BBC Children in Need. These holidays, frequently organised by Neil, a superb Enrolled Nurse, had a greater purpose than fun. They were an opportunity to develop self-care and self-management in our young people, in an environment where peer group pressure and support meant that they took control of their own tablets, injections, and treatments, sometimes for the first time. They also had a cooking rota which led to some very interesting meals!

Neil, in 1988, asked if I would help him in UK recruitment of 10 young people with cystic fibrosis, to travel with us to Canada, to act as Counsellors at a well-established Cystic Fibrosis Summer Camp run by Toronto Sick Children's Hospital. I eagerly agreed. We carefully recruited some amazing young people from all corners of the UK and arranged our six weeks unpaid leave. Arriving at the camp, in the most beautiful location on Lake Couchiching, we were eagerly greeted by the Toronto team, and started our induction into the regimented routine of camp life.

I don't think I ever felt so reservedly British. I disapproved of the total bedlam at mealtimes, with children encouraged to constantly join in chants and songs which ended in people climbing on chairs and running around the room. For example, a chant that was often used went like this: 'X, X if your able, take your elbows off the table. This is not a horse's stable, but a first-class dining table, stand up, stand up, stand up ...' to be followed by being asked to run around the room! To me it certainly didn't encourage calorie intake, which was so vital for these children.

A particularly embarrassing chant that shocked the British children into an embarrassed silence, and that was later, after a quiet word with the Camp Director, banned from use during our stay, ended in the words, '...what a wanker'. In Canada this simply translated to, 'what an idiot'. I left Neil to explain its UK masturbation meaning.

Neil, who had been to the camp many times before, thrived, enjoying the atmosphere and all the outdoor life. I was not as keen, feeling incredibly responsible for the UK young people's welfare. Having never been a sporty person and put off from lake swimming, my one enjoyed activity, by the leeches, I retreated to helping in the camp medical centre.

I do, however, still have fond memories of the quiet time spent with the children and our young people sitting by the lake, or sitting singing around the nightly campfires, and I did try and throw myself into the night entertainment. Neil and my rendition of 'Summer Loving' from Grease was legendary! Each morning at camp everyone gathered around the Canadian flag and, as the flag was raised, gave a moving hand-on-heart rendition of the Canadian National Anthem.

One of our most testing moments was when the lovely Camp Director decided that, in honour of our presence, on one Sunday the camp would sing the British National Anthem. A nice thought, but our UK young people, and indeed Neil, didn't know the British National Anthem! There followed secret meetings of the UK team, with me trying to teach them the words, all in whispers as sound carried across the camp. The Sunday morning dawned, and we gathered around the flag, where I sang a vigorous solo, with Neil's only support a continuous repetition of 'God save Lizzy'!

My time at the camp came to an abrupt halt when one of our 16-year olds, John, became very ill. I ended up resident with him in Toronto Children's Hospital as his parents were unable to fly out because his brother, also with cystic fibrosis, was extremely ill in Bristol. It was a nightmare, stuck in a small isolation room together as we were considered an MRSA risk. Emotions were high and tempers flared, with the frustrated young man shouting and throwing things around the room.

The ward team were very attentive, actually over attentive. They were required by a 'rounding' protocol to come into the room each hour, day and night, so they could tick an observation box. I was exhausted. I also came to hate informal polo shirt uniforms as I had no idea who anyone was. I spent a week thinking the play leader was a doctor as she always entered with a stethoscope around her neck. After a week, a kindly physiotherapist at the camp sent me her flat keys so I could retreat each night to my own space, usually going via the Cadburys shop in the Victoria Centre for a chocolate fix.

Eventually, I convinced the Toronto team that John needed to fly home to be with his parents and dying sibling, and I would accompany him. I returned to the camp to collect essentials for us both and ended up on a night shift in the medical centre with a sick Canadian child!

John and I left the next day on a BA flight but were not welcomed by fellow business class passengers! To give us seats, two German passengers had been forcibly bumped. We boarded to muttered comments and poisonous looks from the other eight members of their party! The atmosphere did not improve when, each time I had to give intravenous medication, the helpful steward decided to put on all the main cabin lights, waking anyone trying to sleep. Disgruntlement reached a peak when, just as all had finally settled for a quiet night, John started to struggle to breathe and I requested Oxygen, not realising this meant dropping the oxygen masks across the whole cabin, permanently waking all!

It felt an incredibly long flight. I have never been so pleased to see a UK ambulance crew when they boarded the plane at Heathrow to help us off. The final insult, for my German 'friends', was having to stay seated until we had disembarked! Once in the ambulance, John again became stroppy, refusing to lie on the trolley, but insisting he sat in a chair, which meant we were short of a seat. The ambulance crew took control, gave me the trolley, and I slept all the way to Bristol.

After handing over to the Bristol team and John's parents, I realised I was now in Bristol on August Bank Holiday Monday, with no easy means of getting back to Manchester! My family were holidaying in Spain so no rescue there! I made my way to Temple Mead Station. Over the next 10 hours I got as far as Crewe, where in desperation I rang a friend of the family, Cath, who nobly came the 30 miles to get me.

When she arrived at Crewe, Cath broke the news that the night before our family home had been broken into, and the police were awaiting my arrival home to identify what had been taken! I arrived to a mess and rapidly tried to identify missing items. A kindly policeman, who had organised the securing of the house, asked if I was Ok to stay there alone, to which my desperate reply was, "If they haven't stolen my bed, I will be fine."

I was shattered. The end of this tale was that, when my parents returned home, I had the pleasure of revisiting the police station to inform them that most of what I had reported stolen my parents had in fact put in the safe before their departure!

Not long after this trip to the Canadian Cystic Fibrosis camp, CF sufferers around the world started to succumb to a new multi-resistant bug, Pseudomonas Cepacia. The death rate soared and contact between CF patients was banned. This in one fair swoop prevented any outings, holidays, or even contact within the ward area with children nursed in isolation. Thank goodness we had introduced home intravenous therapy, as maintaining a fun environment on the ward became difficult for patients and staff. An increasing number of children I had gotten to know so well over the last eight years sadly died and I was to witness time and again the devastation of each family. Anger was common. A parent I had known since their son's diagnosis six years before, on the day of his death beat on my chest.

"I did everything you said and he's dead." It was an intensely upsetting time.

The team made sure that each funeral was attended. This was a true test of professionalism for my young team, controlling their own expressions of grief to enable them to support the family. The open coffin tradition in some Northern towns proved too much for one staff member. The parents rushed to support her, perhaps an indication of how central we had become in these families' lives, but for me a concern.

My mantra to the team was, "We are not their parents." When a child on the ward was dying, yes, we were there to support, but we also had another 18 patients and families to care for, who had their own anxieties and needs. I did, however, envy the staff who could share a silent tear with the parents as a child passed from this life. I never cried on duty, becoming ever more practical and professional. My danger time for a teary meltdown during these years was when curled up on the settee at home watching a sad film on the TV. 'The Student Prince' never failed to leave me a wreck, as he left his love to become king!

My decision to leave this post, which I loved, came after a

particularly traumatic week, when we had four deaths. When comforting a bereaved mother, I realised that I was saying all the right things but my mind was planning the next day's admissions. I was worried that I had distanced myself from the situation, and perhaps time had come to move on.

CHAPTER 4

ACADEMIA AND EDUCATION

- Batchelor of Science in Nursing with Honours (BSc Hons) 1990
- Post Graduate Certificate in Education (PGCE) 1991
- Master of Science (MSc) 1996
- Doctor of Philosophy (PhD) 2004
- Nurse Development Advisor 1991–1992 (Alderhey Children Hospital, Liverpool)
- Senior Lecturer/Practitioner 1993–1997 (Preston)
- Principal Lecturer 1998–1999 (University of Central Lancashire, Preston)
- Dean/Pro Vice Chancellor 2010–2014 (Faculty of Health, London South Bank University)

Awards/Honours:
1998 – Member of the Order of the British Empire (MBE) – for Services to PaediatricHealthcare and Clinical Practice Benchmarking
2014 – Honorary Professor of Nursing at London South Bank University
2014 – Nursing Times Leaders Award
2016 – Honorary Doctor of Nursing at Oxford Brookes University

By the time I was 23, and a ward sister, I knew that to provide the best possible care for the patients and families in my care, the time had come to expand my knowledge of wider health care. I commenced, unbeknown and unsupported by my employer, a part-time nursing degree programme. Although, with juggling full-time shifts, time off became a thing of the past, the timing was right for me. I will never regret not having entered the profession at 18 via a nursing degree programme. Sociology, and social policy lectures on health inequalities, would have meant nothing to my 18-year-old middle-class self.

As a ward sister caring for families from the poorest areas of Manchester, the knowledge I gained was a revelation. I will always be grateful for the excellent pre-registration training I received at Thomas's, and the pride they instilled in me as a Nightingale nurse, but my academic studies, at degree and master's level, developed in me a questioning and analytical approach. This compelled me to always strive to deliver care that was not only based on the latest evidence, but that also took into account the specific needs of each patient and their families.

I graduated in 1990, when graduate nurses were still a rarity, and although in 2009 nursing became a totally graduate profession, many people still sadly ask me why nurses need to have a degree. They seem to totally fail to grasp the complex nature of good nursing care, and the need for nurses to be able to rapidly grasp new knowledge and adapt to new advances in health care. As an example, when I trained in the 1970s, learning about 20 drugs would suffice. If a drug name ended in -one it was a steroid, -illin it was an antibiotic, etc. Now there are thousands of drugs; technology use has exploded, and treatment options are phenomenal. With such complexity, the potential to harm patient we are trying to help is ever increasing. Nursing is certainly a graduate-level profession, and indeed is a profession that demands lifelong learning.

I was to further advance my own education in 1994 when I registered for a masters degree at Liverpool University, narrowly missing out on accessing a clinical nursing masters that was developed the year after. Although at the time I wished I'd waited and accessed the nursing masters, later in my career I was to be grateful that I had completed my masters in the Medical School, with students from a vast array of health professional groups.

The course was very self-directed, with lecturers appearing to be more interested in their own research profile than teaching. Although 30 started only two of us completed. This made delivery in the last year tricky as it was not worth running modules for two. We were initially offered access to any module within the University. This offer was, however, withdrawn when I signed up for a module on snake bites, and instead greater credits were given for an extended thesis. My thesis was on nurse-doctor power relationships in paediatric clinical decision making, and in my later career I know this influenced how I interacted with medical colleagues.

I enjoyed the personal development afforded to me by undertaking my own degree and master's programmes, but my greatest satisfaction has been in developing those around me. On leaving my sisters post in 1990, I decided that I would pursue a career that allowed me to educate the next generation of nurses. I went to London to study my Post Graduate Certificate in Education.

This was the most chilled year of my life! I was fully funded by the nursing English National Board, and one of the Manchester paediatrician's, Lisa, who has remained a close friend, provided me with London accommodation. At first, I lived in her vacant flat, but eventually moved in with her parents. They needed a regular house and dog sitter, to allow them to frequently travel to their house in Ireland. When they were in residence the house was constantly filled with musicians and arty types.

It was an artistic world I had never before encountered. Calming violinist who were in tears because their vibrato was not quite right, and discussing the vagaries of modern art, were regular events. I found it not only stimulating but such fun. When Lisa's parents were away, Dinah, the elderly standard poodle, was my company. My priorities during these times were preventing Dinah from eating the post and making sure she got precisely 13 chocolate drops each evening.

Life was unbelievably stress free. I had never had the joy of being a full-time student, having started nursing and shift work from 18, and doing my degree whilst a full-time ward sister. A particular highlight was experiencing for the first time Universities' Wednesday's sport afternoon. A group of us very seriously addressed the challenge created by a voluntary module, Shakespearean pubs of London!

There were 60 students in our year from all walks of life, and from around the world.

Only six of us were nurses, so during the assessed peer teaching I learnt how to fold serviettes into a swan; about four-wheel drive suspension; how to rig a yacht, etc …

The nurse I became very friendly with was one of the international students, Angela. She was a Swaziland nurse tutor, whose government had given her only a few days warning of her enforced departure to undertake this teachers' training course in London. If she had refused to come, she would have lost her job and her family's only income. She had left behind her four children, the youngest being under six months old.

Angela arrived in a cold September, with no jumpers or coats, and with no knowledge of the UK. She was a larger than life, jolly lady, whose laugh would light up a room. Once we had sorted appropriate attire for the UK weather for her, I had great fun showing her the sights, and watching her excitement at every new experience.

In North Wales, when a bit thirsty she tried to drink the sea, as coming from a country with no coast she had no idea it was salty. In the Lake District her shrieks of delight on the Windermere Ferry, her first time on a boat, were a joy to fellow passengers. My favourite memory was taking her to see 'Miss Saigon' at a London theatre. It opened with a street scene, seen through a sheer curtain. When the curtain was raised, Angela, who had decided, because of the screen, that we had come to a movie, jumped from her seat.

"It's real, it's real," she screamed in delight.

There followed in a loud voice a running commentary of all the action. Fellow London theatre goers were not amused!

Teaching practice at an outer London school of nursing was a nightmare for Angela.

The unhelpful, and I still think unkind and probably racist staff, allocated her teaching sessions that were totally unreasonable and impossible for her, for example, around UK sociology. Within a month she lost over a stone from stress. She was unwilling to complain, as she knew failure was not an option for her government sponsor.

I was furious and asked the course tutor to talk to Angela's link nurse training school to request Angela was allocated more appropriate sessions e.g., basic physiology. She refused, so for any sessions Angela was likely to struggle with, I stepped in to write her lesson plans and slides. She was a highly intelligent individual, and she survived and returned home to take up a nurse training leadership position in Swaziland. We have sadly never met again, but I often think about her and how much observing her experience and treatment taught me about the importance of mutual respect and the impact of discrimination.

My own teaching practice was at the Charles West School in Great Ormond Street Children's Hospital (GOSH). This was a doddle for me, especially when compared to the experience of the non-nursing students, working in inner London Further Education (FE) colleges. We used to debrief each week, and they would describe the abuse and violence they were subjected to; threatened with knives, cars overturned, and a generally terrifying introduction to teaching. At GOSH student nurses still stood when tutors entered the room.

Another big advantage of being placed at GOSH was the local parking fee. I never had a full assessment of any of my teaching sessions, as the assessing lecturer was not prepared to put any more than £1 in the metre, which lasted her 20 minutes (20p for four minutes). This tutor was an unusual lady. She arrived in class one day in tears because her two vegetarian Rottweilers had eaten her cat!

The GOSH tutors were a dedicated but quite old-fashioned group, spending lunchtimes sharing embroidery and needlepoint tips. The exception was, thankfully, my supervisor, who rescued me most days to lunch at the local fry up café, or the pub.

Working again with children and families was a delight, but what was difficult was the GOSH handmaiden approach to working with the consultants. The medical control was absolute, and it reached a tipping point for me when, one day, one of the students was told to lie to a parent of a child with newly diagnosed cystic fibrosis. The consultant was skiing, and no one was allowed to inform the parents of the diagnosis until his return. In the interim, the nurses were told to tell the family that the vital pancreatic enzyme tablets were vitamins. Having spent eight years as the sister on a cystic fibrosis ward in Manchester, where the ethos was truth, I was furious that it was felt appropriate to teach new nurses to lie. With my supervisor's support I threatened to withdraw all the students from the ward, which would have led to closure, as in those days student nurses were the backbone of a ward nursing rota. The senior registrar stepped in and told the family the truth.

In educational terms, the greatest challenge of teaching at GOSH was making sure the student nurses would be able to pass a general paediatric state finals exam, when their only clinical experience was with children suffering from the rarest of conditions. As an experienced paediatric nurse, however, I thoroughly enjoyed being confronted with the daily challenge of specialisation. What I could not cope with was the god-like treatment of doctors and the subservience expected from nursing. On my last day, the head of the school asked me to return as a tutor at the end of my teacher training. I declined the offer, flippantly saying that I would only return when I was one of the bosses, a prediction that was to come true.

My original plan on obtaining my Post Graduate Certificate in Education was to return to teach in Manchester. However, as my course was coming to an end, I was approached by my previous Director of Nursing in Manchester. She asked if I would move with her to Alder Hey Children's Hospital in Liverpool, to develop in-service training for nurses. I was delighted to move back up North, but Liverpool, only 60 miles from Manchester, was a totally different environment.

On my first day I was shown around this sizable hospital, including all the vast array of outpatient clinics, and on making my way back down the long central corridor a mother, with a sullen-looking toddler, stopped me.

"Can you tell me where the clinic is?" she asked in a broad scouse accent. Proud of my new knowledge I sought clarification.

"Which clinic are you wanting?" She looked vague, so I continued, "Is it his eyes, ears, head, leg …?"

After a pause she responded, "It's his arse."

Ah yes, the arse clinic, always difficult to find!

Some children on the long-stay wards were very reluctant to talk to someone with a 'posh' accent; I recall one occasion when, to convince one 12-year-old to converse with me, for the first time in my life I started watching Coronation Street, her favourite soap!

The job itself was a gift as there had been very little post-registration training available for nurses, and they enthusiastically attended every offered opportunity. My office was, however, a nightmare, a small room over the kitchen area which so badly reeked of frying fat it made me gag. I could see why it had been available!

I was thoroughly enjoying my practice development post when, due to serious issues in the Cardiac and Intensive Care Directorate, I was asked to move across to a management position. I think I felt flattered, and foolishly accepted this new flight path. The turbulence experienced in this management role I will describe later, but for now suffice to say that three years later I decided to leave Alder Hey to return to academia. I took a drop in salary to commence a dream job as a paediatric lecturer practitioner in Preston, based between the Royal Preston Hospital and the University of Central Lancashire.

It was at the Royal Preston that I met Kathy, my manager for the 50% practitioner part of the role. She was to become a close friend. I discovered, from day one, her kind and caring nature, when, after work, she took me and a colleague out to a welcome dinner at an Italian restaurant. I didn't dare own up to a developing migraine and after the main meal I became very unwell. Having vomited and fainted, Kathy, realising I lived 20 miles away down the M6, drove me to her nearby house so I could collapse into bed. It was not until fully recovered in the morning that I realised it was a one-bedroom house. She had given me her bed, spending the night herself on a bed chair! So embarrassing, but certainly the way to get to know each other, and indeed our friendship continued to grow and between 1998 to 2004 we shared a house.

This house sharing arrangement came about due to a burglary. One lovely summer's evening, a group of us had decided to go to the open-air theatre in Lancaster to see Midsummer Night's Dream. Driving Kathy home afterwards, we found that her rented house had been ransacked, and her car, just two days old, had been stolen from the drive.

Having dealt with the police, Kathy was not safe to stay in her insecure rented house, so I drove us both to my house, and we shared my house for the next two years, eventually buying a house together.

It was a great arrangement as we got on so well, and together we could afford a lovely home, but from 1999 I was working between Leeds and London, so was rarely in residence. When Kathy retired in 2004 she moved nearer to her family and our house was sold. Kathy has continued to be my closest friend but in those first few years of our acquaintance she taught me so much about effective and compassionate management.

Working with such a supportive manager became particularly important when, for the first time in my life, I was to discover how bullying could turn me from a very confident, effective professional to a crying wreck. For reasons I will never truly understand, early in my time as a lecturer practitioner, my manager for the 50% University time started to undermine every statement I made in meetings, repeatedly pulling me aside to tell me in quiet corners that my colleagues hated working with me. I started to feel more and more isolated, and totally dreaded my University days.

It came to a head one day, when, about to leave the wards for a meeting with this University manager, Kathy, sensing something was wrong, asked if I was OK. I burst into tears, something I had never ever done at work. Through my sobs I shared with her what was going on. She immediately set up a meeting with the University Head of HR. Within a day I was reporting to a new excellent University manager, and over the next week, although I had said nothing to University colleagues, two of them sought me out to tell me that they had suffered similar bullying from this manager.

I have often tried to analyse why this situation occurred. When I consider the three of us chosen to be the focus of her bullying activity, we were all very sociable, likeable, and lively individuals, and perhaps there was an element of jealousy. I have no idea what disciplinary action was taken against the manager, but no formal statements were ever taken. She continued to work, but with a reduced team. She was an extremely bright and believable individual and did later hold quite a senior national position. I avoided all future contact.

I can only hope that, despite my distressed mental state at the time and choosing not to formally pursue a complaint, she also learnt from these events. As to me, although horrific at the time, I am actually grateful for the insight this incident gave me into the destructive power of bullying. One person's behaviour turned me from a happy, effective professional to a blithering, indecisive idiot. I believe that it has made me a far better manager. I am extremely sensitive to early signs of bullying in my teams, and certainly have zero tolerance to any bullying or discriminatory behaviour.

Once this situation was resolved, the lecturer practitioner post itself was the best of all worlds. I could, with no management responsibilities, continue to work directly with the children and families at the same time as educating my colleagues and the students who were starting their paediatric nursing career.

I was seen as the person to go to for clinical supervision and advice, even if inappropriate timing! On a memorable occasion, a terrified staff nurse came rushing towards me to help set up the ventilator for a child who was urgently awaiting a flying squad retrieval from the Liverpool paediatric intensive care unit. The child was stabilised, and it was only then that the staff nurse was embarrassed to notice that I was in a nightie and dressing gown, dragging with me an IV stand and catheter bag. I'd had an appendicectomy two days before on the ward below, and I'd only come up to see if Kathy was around! The parents looked equally bemused by the sight of a 'patient' setting up their child's breathing machine.

It was humbling to be considered the one who could provide the answers when nurses were faced with difficult clinical situations. Calls even came in the middle of the night, including a three a.m. call to help with a violent teenager high on drugs. This highlighted to me how every experience in life is of future worth, as over that night I relied on the knowledge and skills gleaned in my brief sojourn in child psychiatry at the age of 19.

One event that challenged me whilst at Preston was to have a profound impact on my life, leading to my undertaking doctoral studies and becoming a senior civil servant in Whitehall.

I have always been a great believer in teamwork and sharing and have certainly had a 'not reinventing the wheel' approach. What I have never been able to understand is why people don't freely share their good ideas. This came to a head for me when the team at Preston were struggling to control the pain of an 18-month-old burns patient, who had pulled a kettle of boiling water on herself. As the Lecturer/Practitioner at the time, my help was sought to control her unrelenting pain, and I reached out to the children's hospitals across the UK for advice. Some shamefully refused to share without payment, but others immediately sent across all the guidance and procedures they used. Following these, this little girl's agony was gradually lessened.

At the time I was a clinical frontline member of the English Chief Nursing Officers Practice Advisory Group, and at a meeting we had had a talk on benchmarking. I decided this was exactly what we needed to establish. Within a week I had set up a paediatric clinical practice benchmarking group, with membership from 12 hospitals and three Universities from across the North West of England. We immediately started collaborating and formally sharing good practice.

The meetings were inspirational, and I became passionate about exploring how effective clinical practice benchmarking really was in actually improving the quality of patient care.

This became the question to be answered throughout my PhD studies. The next seven years were a rollercoaster. As will be described in chapter five, I was, as a civil servant, able to use emerging findings from my research but, with no study leave from commencement to conclusion, juggling time to complete my PhD was a nightmare. A large amount of my analysis, and the writing up, was undertaken on train journeys or on holidays with friends. For seven years I never read a novel but became an avid reader of quality improvement articles and 'Statistics Made Simple'!

At last, in 2003, I was ready to submit and face the dreaded viva. One of my supervisors accompanied me to take copious notes of the discussion and the feedback given. I, and my observing supervisor, were delighted when we were given only one page of comments and the examiners informed me that only minor amendments were needed. We celebrated with my Director of Studies, and his young daughter handed me a congratulations card that she had made. When people asked how it had gone, I said it had gone well but I had minor changes to make.

I was, therefore, staggered, distraught, and embarrassed when, about two weeks later, I received a letter from the University saying that, on reflection, and when completing the examiners form, the external examiner had actually not ticked the minor or major amendments box but that I was being offered an MPhil. Devastated,

I immediately contacted the supervisor and Director of Studies who were furious. I decided to appeal even though I was told by the University that there was no point as I could only appeal on procedural grounds.

It was at this point a friend, Linda, who was a Nursing Professor at University College London, rallied to support me. We gathered all the evidence, the notes taken, statements from the supervisor, the card given, and most powerfully the very minimal changes that had been requested. Linda then accompanied me to the appeal hearing. At the hearing I managed, with difficulty, to make my case in a calm and professional manner. The Vice Chancellor kept repeating I could only 'win' if there were proven procedural errors, the suggestion being that it was hopeless. It was of interest that when the hearing was over and Linda and I were sitting outside to recover, that two members of the appeal panel came to personally, but confidentially, apologise to me. This really infuriated Linda.

I won the appeal and was resent the changes required to be awarded the PhD. These exactly matched the minor changes originally discussed and noted by my observing supervisor. It took only two months to complete the required changes to the satisfaction of the internal examiner, and my PhD was awarded.

I still do not understand what happened. My friends wondered if there was an element of professional jealousy from the external examiner. I was the Director of Nursing at GOSH and she apparently held an inconsequential academic position in a university.

Although this was a horrible experience, it certainly informed my own future academic behaviour. As a PhD supervisor and examiner, I was always honest with students, recognizing the prolonged effort of completing a PhD and the incredible stress of a viva.

In 2016 I was honoured to be made an Honorary Doctor of Nursing at Oxford Brookes University, an event I enjoyed far more than my own PhD graduation event. This time there was no undercurrent of injustice, just a celebration of what I had achieved over 38 years in the nursing profession.

Although my PhD experience in 2004 does not reflect well on UCLan, my earlier time working there was valuable. By the time I left, in 1999, I was a Principal Lecturer, leading the children's nursing team. I had started to really understand the full complexity of Higher Education Institutions. We were a small, highly effective, and dedicated team, delivering paediatric training from pre-registration to advanced practice level, and travelling to University sites across the northwest.

We all loved our jobs and the only reward we required was the success of our students. I was therefore rather amazed when, in 1998, I received a letter from Buckingham Palace asking if I would accept an Honour from the Queen, a Member of the Order of the British Empire (MBE). The envelope was not that impressive, and I was convinced that it was a prank initiated by one of the fun-loving Enrolled Nurses on the paediatric wards. I thought it was her retaliation for a joke letter we had sent to her, an avid Coronation Street fan, saying that she had been chosen to be an extra in the Rovers Return pub. It was only when I saw her baffled expression, when I confronted her, that I realised the Honours letter was real and rushed home to retrieve it from the bin!

You never know who nominated you and keeping my honour a secret for six weeks was really tricky. Eventually on June 15th, which happened to be my mother's birthday, it was announced. The congratulatory letters received from not only the great and the good, but also from colleagues and families I had cared for, were overwhelming. Mum, Dad, and Jane were to accompany me, but when the date arrived Jane announced that she would be on a family holiday. She insisted that I ring the palace to ask for a new date! This was one of the strangest, and probably most embarrassing, phone calls of my life. It was obviously expected that dates of invitations from the Queen were just eagerly accepted.

However, pleading family commitments, I was allowed to delay until the November.

The day arrived and, dressed in our finery, we had the unique pleasure of asking a London cabby to take us into Buckingham Palace. The first disaster was, as I was separated from the family and directed up a flight of impressive steps, I tripped and to break my fall grabbed onto a passing palace guard who valiantly remained statuesque, as I spluttered an apology. Then came the greater embarrassment. Having moved the date I realised at the briefing that I was to be first of the civilian recipients, following on from the military, who had all been rehearsing for weeks! Prince Charles was presenting us with our awards, and we were firmly instructed on when to pause, when to turn, curtsy, walk forward, speak, shake hands, back away, curtsy again, and then walk away. I managed the approach with some degree of decorum, but when Prince Charles had shaken my hand, I automatically turned my back to walk away. I was instantly aware of my error.

I spontaneously muttered, "Oh shit," and then, realising my gaffe, followed this with, "Sorry," apologetically grabbing Prince Charles's arm. This then led me into a further flurry of sorrys, before I shuffled away with haste.

I tried to immediately forget this embarrassment, but unfortunately the University treated me to the video of my MBE investiture, on which, if you watch carefully, you can lip read my faux pas, but you can also see Prince Charles's amusement.

I think one of the reasons that I came to the attention of the civil service as a potential recruit was the MBE and, in 1999, I left UCLan.

In 2010, I returned to educating the next generation of health professionals but took on a wider focus when I became the Dean of Health at London South Bank University, the largest health faculty in the UK with around 7,000 students. There were the usual challenges of validations, tender bids, contracting and research assessment exercises, but the senior team had all angles covered, and the faculty went from strength to strength. As Dean, my role was focused around negotiating with commissioners and making sure that London South Bank was the University of choice for not only students, but also for partner hospitals.

Quality training mattered, but I was only too aware that I was now running a highly profitable business. To expand I became increasingly involved in external facing activity, which included managing and trying to develop more international income streams. My travel partner for these endeavours was usually Mary. She had for many years been supporting radiography programmes in Hong Kong and Singapore, and our travels always included attendance at degree ceremonies in these locations.

On one memorable occasion we had commenced our trip in India. The temperature was over 50 degrees centigrade and, due to lightning strikes, there were widespread power failures. Fridges and air conditioning units were not working, and sadly neither were lifts. I remember climbing 15 flights of stairs to discuss vocational training with government officials. We commenced our climb, smart and cool, and arrived in the room breathless and soaking wet with sweat. A tricky look when trying to appear professional.

As always in India, everywhere we went we were offered Indian snacks, and at one hot meeting I foolishly accepted a chicken skewer. Mary sensibly remained vegetarian. We flew out of India to a far cooler Singapore the day after, and it was only when we were on the pristine subway system I succumbed to campylobacter, a vomiting bug. I will never forget Mary's horrified look when I announced I was about to be sick. This diminutive lady manhandled me off the subway and up the escalator at the next stop to find a convenient bush, saying all the way,

"Not now, not in Singapore."

I had one day to recover before our Radiographers degree ceremony, and only made it by hanging onto the lectern whilst shaking hands.

The next day we flew on to Hong Kong for the next ceremony. Three days later, and much recovered, I decided I could fancy, as my first meal, steamed dim sum! It was evening and we enquired at the hotel reception where we could find evening dim sum, usually a lunch time delicacy. The receptionist directed us to the passages underneath the train station. Having weaved our way underground, we found ourselves in an area only populated by locals, and there was the dim sum café. About 30 people were queuing in three rows. We joined a row. We were handed a form in Chinese, and having absolutely no clue what we were ordering, ticked a few boxes. Once our order had been handed in at the cash desk, the cashier wrote something on a slip of paper that she gave us and we were ushered to stand in another area.

We then realised the symbols on the form was our number, but we had no idea what it said. As 'numbers' were called out people found seats on long trestle tables, sharing pots of tea, and their food arrived. After a very short time we realised a number kept being repeated, but nobody was moving, and gradually people turned to look at us. Eventually, a young girl took the form from Mary, and nodded to us to go forward. We joined a crowded table, and with great excitement opened our first dim sum basket to find a dish of chicken feet, inedible to us, but gratefully received when we donated them to our neighbours. We were relieved that the remainder of our baskets were delicious!

Food was a bit of a theme on our trips. My first trip to China, to visit our Chinese partners for our acupuncture master's programme, started with a Chinese banquet. We had travelled non-stop from the UK to Harbin in Northern China and were desperate for sleep, but when we landed, we were taken with great ceremony to a restaurant. On the table were individual bowls of watery soup, each placed over a small warming candle. Then in came the live delicacies; prawns waving antennae; fish still flapping; and small eels wiggling around a dish. My neighbour demonstrated skewering an eel, which was then plunged into the soup to die. As a good Northerner used to eating offal and eels, much to Mary's horror, I entered into the spirit of the occasion.

"How long does an eel take to die?" I asked my neighbour.

Mary became vegetarian!

Harbin was an incredible experience. We awoke on the first morning to a military-style parade in the square outside our window. Having been collected by our Chinese escorts, our first stop was a visit to a hospital ward. It was full of patients covered in numerous acupuncture needles. The pharmacy, our next stop, was the size of a large warehouse, full of plants and with numerous large bubbling cauldrons.

The Harbin visit was, however, not all work. We were honoured to be given a private tour of a museum containing the most beautiful hand-illustrated first-century-BC herbology journals. The most amusing outing was on our last day, when our Chinese escorts decided to take us to the Siberia Tiger Park.

It was a surreal experience with humans driven around in cages, and tigers running free. It was very busy, and Mary was sat in the last remaining outward-facing bench seat by the door opening. Her seat was the only one in the cage that did not benefit from four-foot plastic panels, the importance of which was about to become clear. The cage vehicle slowly drove around the park, stopping at one point to watch tigers plunging into a lake and chasing after and slaughtering sacrificed live ducks. We were relieved to move on to a less harrowing tiger observation stop, but then I suddenly heard a commotion from the door area. The tigers were in turn reversing up to the cage, raising their tails and directing copious, extremely pungent urine directly at the unscreened Mary. She was dripping in tiger wee. Although I cruelly found this hysterical, I found it less amusing when I realised we were to be driven straight to the airport to fly back to Beijing. Mary managed a quick change and baby wipe wash in the airport toilet but failed to remove the stench. It was a smelly flight, and we made no friends!

Mary and I did try to have a half day exploring wherever we happened to be. One of our regular destinations was Sarawak, where we were trying to work in partnership with a Kuching nurse training school to help train nurses. Borneo is very beautiful, and one afternoon our host suggested taking us to visit the Sarawak Cultural Village. On arrival, it was with horror I realised that to enter we were required to cross a bamboo swing bridge. I have always been terrified of heights! Mary strode across and I set off with conviction, but , as the bridge began to swing, I froze and ended up crawling on all fours to the end, where Mary and our guide were creased up laughing. Mary had resisted taking a photograph for which I was grateful, but I was less grateful when the guide said we could have used the disabled access ramp! Having regained my decorum, we set off with fascination to see the houses on stilts. This was the next challenge for my acrophobia, as to get onto the 10-foot-high platform you were required to use triangular wedge steps which had no handrail or support. As I was deciding entry for me was impossible, hands grabbed me from above and below and I was manhandled up. It was certainly worth the embarrassment, and I wandered through the rooms, entertained by local musicians and craft artists. It was only on reaching the exit that I realised it was a ramp that I could have come up!

Your travel companion on business trips matters a great deal, not only for business success, but to provide the vigour to fully engage with your hosts, as it is exhausting to be constantly on show and analysing every interaction. Mary and I were perfectly matched, and the University benefited and so did we, forming a friendship that will last.

We can both tell many stories, but this was a team that worked. In most of the countries we visited, senior positions were male dominated, and we learnt the importance of using our Professorial titles at every opportunity. On one flight, with Royal Brunei Air, this title game served us particularly well. At check in we discovered, with excitement, that we had been upgraded from business class to First Class. Having partaken of a chef-prepared meal in the First-Class Lounge, we went to board the plane, passing two sniffer dogs on the passenger boarding bridge. On presenting our boarding passes at the door, there followed an excited exchange between the stewardesses, but we carried on past them to find our seats. As the plane filled, it became evident that we were the only females in First Class, and, sensing that this was causing great consternation, we smiled sweetly and settled into our seats.

As the doors were about to shut, in came a young boy of about 12, a smartly dressed middle-aged man, and four very large muscular men. They looked shocked to see us, and there followed further unintelligible conversations, but eventually all settled, and the plane took off. Being newcomers to First Class, the gadgets caused Mary some confusion, and once the seat belt sign had been turned off, she called down to me to ask if I had sussed how to release the TV screen. The young boy, who was directly next to her, jumped from his seat to help, and as he arose so did the four muscle men. In perfect English he guided Mary through use of the screen, and all five retook their seats. She then called for help with her table, and again he, plus the four, came to her rescue. Newspapers were then passed around, and Mary, thinking that the young boy may be interested in her rejected sports pages, started to pass them across the aisle to him. The four muscle men jumped up, and grabbed the paper, shouting at the boy who recoiled into his seat. Having checked the paper, it was handed to him. The flight then continued, with occasional visits from women from Business Class who talked to the boy and cast us poisonous looks. The mystery was solved when we arrived in London to be informed that we must remain in our seats whilst the Crown Prince's party disembarked. Professors in Brunei are obviously male!

My time at London South Bank University (LSBU) sadly ended in 2014 due to repeated clashes with a newly appointed Vice Chancellor over the future of the Health Faculty. I had for the previous three and a half years, under the previous VC, been allowed, and indeed encouraged, to develop the Faculty systems and structure in any way the Faculty team felt would benefit the London health service, and the business of the University. We had been highly successful. Recruitment was high with no need to enter clearing for nursing. Relationships with commissioners and health service partners were excellent. This was largely as I had been a fellow Director of Nursing prior to taking the job, and they knew I understood their requirements. Contracts with hospitals were eagerly signed, and the Faculty income was, each year, able to subsidise the underperforming Faculties. I really enjoyed my role. I felt truly appreciated and respected by the VC and senior university colleagues, as well as NHS colleagues, and was honoured to receive a Nursing Times Leaders Award in 2014.

Then came the new Vice Chancellor, eager to put his mark on the University, and seemingly hell bent on uniformity of structures and systems across the University. To begin with I tried to defend why the Faculty of Health functioned as it did, but it became clear I was not to be heard, and change was to be enforced. Some changes I recognised would have minimal negative impact on the Faculty's success, for example changing its name to a school. However, in some areas, which I felt would be disastrous for business, I was prepared to fight. The VC just didn't want to listen. Our relationship deteriorated. One Friday I tried to explain to the VC why centralizing administration and placement functions would not work for complex nursing training placements. His emailed response, received on a

Saturday morning, basically said 'I don't care what you think. Just do as you are told.' I was totally insulted and furious, but realising that this conflict was not helping anyone, including my team, and having to accept that he was the boss, I knew that I had to leave.

Within three weeks I had applied for and had been offered the Chief Executive Officer post at the Royal College of Paediatrics and Child Health. I left LSBU, having accepted an Honorary Professorial post to allow me to continue the supervision of my PhD students. I said a sad, and in a way a guilty farewell to my excellent LSBU colleagues, who I felt I was abandoning.

Many of the LSBU team have remained friends but, since my departure, I have had minimal contact with the University. I do still make use of my honorary title to support my global leadership activity, as such titles are of value in opening doors to advance the international recognition of nursing as a respected profession.

CHAPTER 5

CIVIL SERVICE

• Nursing Officer 1999–2002, UK Department of Health (DOH)

One of the first books I was given as a child was the small Penguin book on Florence Nightingale. I can't remember the giver, but I can remember my fascination with the central character. As I matured, the appeal of the image of her walking through wards of the sick, carrying her lamp, developed into an admiration of a young woman who challenged the social norms of her upbringing. A woman who did not hesitate to go into battle with powerful men to improve the lot of others. As I entered further and further into the world of nursing, I increasingly recognised that every nurse has their own day-to-day challenges to overcome, or even battles to fight, if they truly want to ensure a high-quality health service for all.

In the early days of my career, the challenge was around personal knowledge and competence, but all too soon I came to realise that my greatest frustration would be the boundaries enforced by others, or by the system within which I was trying to practice. I again took inspiration from Florence Nightingale, recognising in the letters she wrote from the Crimea to Sidney Herbert, the Secretary of State for War, in 1855, many of the same frustrations that nurses experience today.

The final lecture on leaving the Nightingale School at St. Thomas's Hospital was, in many ways, a call to arms. We were compelled to accept as our vocation our role in going out into the world to transform health care systems.

I was enthused by this challenge to develop not only my own but also others' day-to-day nursing practice. However, as time passed, I realised that I had not truly grasped the depth of the challenge I had been given as a Nightingale nurse. Health care transformation could not be achieved without system change, and to change the system required me to engage in politics and policy development, not just at local but at national level.

My opening at national level came when, in 1993, I was invited to join the Chief Nursing Officer for England's Practice Advisory Group. This group of inspiring nurses was part of the CNO's attempt to really grasp the challenges being faced by nurses on the NHS frontline. I am not sure how useful this group really was for the CNO, but membership certainly redirected my career. I was invited to join in with projects on clinical supervision for nurses, and to work as a civil service secondee on the introduction of nurse prescribing, recommended in 1986 by Baroness Cumberlege.

As an experienced ward sister, not being able to prescribe had been a continuous frustration. I had, when our children with long-term conditions were admitted, spent many hours dictating to junior doctors the drugs that needed to be prescribed, always wishing I could just pick up a pen. This was especially annoying when, on visiting children with cystic fibrosis at home, it was obvious certain drugs were needed. This involved driving back to the hospital, explaining to a helpful doctor what was required, having the prescription written and dispensed, and then driving back to the child's home. Frustrating but also a delay in care. It seemed so clear to me that a legislative change was needed, but what I was to learn was that any policy change attracts dissent. Pharmacists were unhappy, doctors reluctant, and nurses hesitant. It was not until 1998, 12 years after the Cumberlege report, that community nurses were allowed to prescribe from a very limited formulary. I was so disappointed. Being able to prescribe leg ulcer bandages and incontinence pads was of littleuse to a paediatric nurse.

My civil service boss reassured me that full nurse prescribing will happen, but not just yet. "There will be a right time."

He was right, and, in 2006, four years after I'd left the Department of Health, nurse prescribers were given full access to the British National Formulary. I still feel exhilarated when I realise that there are now over 54,000 nurse and midwife prescribers across the UK. I am grateful to my colleagues who took on this challenge and patiently saw it through to delivery. They taught me the need for calm determination and patience when seeking legislative change.

My challenge as a full-time senior civil servant was from 1999 to be at a very different pace. In Tony Blair's leader's speech in 1997, he focused on 'Getting the Basics Right' which, although initially referring to literacy and numeracy, was interpreted by Department of Health colleagues as also including consideration of the quality of basic health services. In July 1998, the consultation document, 'A first-class service – quality in the NHS', provided further detail on the government's plans to tackle quality variation in the health service. National standards were to be published and then monitored through a new Commission for Healthcare Improvement (CHI), a national performance assessment framework and a national patient survey. 'Czars' were appointed to set out national standards in national service frameworks for medical specialties, but nurses in the Department knew that what really mattered to patients was the quality of face-to-face interaction and care.

It was at this point in 1998 that I was approached to join the DoH quality team. I was happily working and living in the North-west of England, and, as described in chapter four, was running the North-west paediatric clinical practice benchmarking group. The Assistant CNO, a paediatric nurse and one of my former managers, was on our steering group, and she had recognised that the patient-focused clinical practice benchmarking approach, that I had developed, may provide the solution the DoH required to improve basic nursing care.

In 1999 I joined the civil service, and over the next three years I was to not only lead the development of the Essence of Care benchmarking toolkit, but to also become involved in many other quality care initiatives.

My own life went on hold. At 5:20 a.m. each Monday morning, I travelled from near Blackpool to Leeds on the Trans Pennine Express. 'Express' was a misnomer! I think it was the slowest train in the UK! I worked all day in Quarry House, the DoH Leeds headquarters, and at 15:50 caught the London train. Tuesday and

Wednesday were usually London based, in the attic of Richmond House in Whitehall, and then Thursday and Friday I travelled around the UK to visit NHS facilities, often not arriving home until after 10 p.m. on Friday.

I was an expert at two-to-three-star hotel living. I learnt how impossible it is to settle with cold feet and thus the value of packing a small hot water bottle, the need for a plug-in bright light to counter awful hotel room lighting and, after incurring major and repetitive expense, to always check I repacked my phone charger. Each week I returned home exhausted, spent Saturday recovering from the weekly migraine, and slept most of Sunday, preparing for the 4:30 alarm on Monday. Reflecting now this sounds an awful existence, but I loved every minute (except perhaps the migraines), and I learnt so much, not just about how the government worked, but also about myself.

In the first 18 months, until its launch in February 2001, developing the Essence of Care toolkit was certainly the main focus of my life. I commissioned literature and research reviews to identify evidence-based best practice in eight areas of patient care, and then, working with a superb colleague, Sandra, travelled the country, to facilitate eight three-day residential workshops. We brought together, in remote hotels, relevant health care professionals and interested patients and carers. On the first evening, the service users were supported in sharing their own, sometimes harrowing, experiences of healthcare.

Then the focus was flipped.

All present were asked to arrive the next morning with their wish list for what would, in their personal or professional view, constitute the very best possible care or practice, informed by what they had shared or heard, and the literature reviews that they had received two weeks before the meeting. Over the next two days these lists were the basis of discussions that allowed us to arrive at agreed patient-focused best practice benchmarks. Recognising the limited funding and thus time, Sandra and I worked late into the night, or occasionally all night, to type up each day's notes so that we could continuously move forward.

We always left the three days with a draft benchmarking document ready to go to wide consultation. Thousands of comments were received, carefully considered, and, if appropriate, incorporated. After 12 months, we had produced a benchmarking toolkit which could support a structured approach to comparison and sharing of good practice. Then came the hurdle of sign off by civil servants and finally, 19 submissions later, by Ministers. The politicians and civil servants had to be convinced that asking nurses to implement the identified good practice was not going to require increased NHS funding, but was more about better education and an appropriate redirection of already available resources.

When launched in 2001, I accepted without question that, as a civil servant, my name would not appear in the publication, and that there would be no mention of my leadership of this initiative. What I found harder to bear was that, on the day of the official launch with the great and the good, I was coldly informed that I was to remain in Leeds to man the phones, so that all my senior colleagues could attend. My secretary bought us celebratory donuts to eat at our desks.

I remember reassuring colleagues that this lack of recognition for so many hours of personal commitment did not concern me. I lied, but it did teach me a lesson for managing others; that you must always acknowledge and never ever take the credit for others' work. What this final insult never took away from me was the pride in what we had produced.

The Essence of Care toolkit was, for those nurses and organisations who grasped its potential, a huge success, really making a difference to patient care, and benchmarks for further areas of practice were released in 2010.

The most inspiring element of working on the Essence of Care toolkit was working with patients and carers. I identified who to invite to attend the workshops from authors of complaint letters that had been sent directly to the health Ministers, the Secretary of State, and the Prime Minister, and from lists of interested parties and complainants provided by the Community Health Councils. The personal stories were often upsetting, but absolutely invaluable. The patients and carers had no hesitation in identifying not only what would be best practice, but making it clear what may block achieving it. When I am on wards today, and see 'do not enter' pegs on curtains, I remember one patient who, when we were discussing privacy and dignity of patients, said,

"When you are sitting on a commode, nurses come through curtains to chat to their friends because they are thoughtless. Doctors come in because they see it as their right."

The need for all care to be patient-, not professional- focused, was the guiding principle of all the benchmarks, and I learnt how to ensure patient voice took precedence over professional protectionism, and indeed pomposity.

My skills at facilitating meaningful engagement with patients, and the public, were recognised by the quality team, and my role further expanded to ensure patient involvement in many more Department of Health quality initiatives. This included, from 2001, supporting patient involvement in the Better Hospital Food project, led by Lloyd Grossman. This was a strange group of very well-meaning individuals, including, as well as two patients and myself, the NHS estates team, the agony aunt and former nurse Claire Raynor, and a delightful Egon Ronay food taster. I always feel disappointed for Lloyd, and rather fatalistic that things will never change, when over subsequent years I see yet another celebratory chef entering the hospital food fray.

Lloyd led this work with such commitment and passion, touring hospitals, meeting hospital chefs, tasting some hideous food, and appealing for a realistic per patient budget, but as he publicly stated at the end, "The team had a number of successes, but their efforts were hampered by a lack of political will."

What I will personally always remember are the meals he took the team to as a thank you for our efforts. I, and the patient reps, visited restaurants in London that we certainly could not have afforded, and would not have known existed as they were too posh to have a sign! Walking in with Lloyd, and the Egon Ronay taster, guaranteed excellence in food and service, although portion size was certainly not Northern!

Working as a senior civil servant was a strange mix. Day-to-day work involved learning a totally new language and way of working. Documents arrived in different coloured 'jackets' depending upon their importance or security level, and each night my desk had to be cleared to abide by the strictly enforced 'clear desk policy'. This is a discipline that I have continued throughout my ongoing career, and which others tell me makes me appear calm and in control. They never see what is crammed into locked drawers!

I was taught how to effectively speed-read vast documents, and to prepare succinct two-page summaries and reports. All invaluable transferable skills. The most challenging, and indeed scary task I had to master, was how to present briefings to support Ministers in answering parliamentary questions in the House of Commons, which included guessing what supplementary questions may be asked. Parliamentary Questions are submitted three days in advance, but by the time they reached my desk, or more frequently my portable laptop, time was always short. It also seemed that health questions were often urgent, with only 24 hours' notice required. The first time this happened, I was on a train, and my civil service boss laughed when I said I needed library time to investigate the answer. He informed me that I was employed for my background expertise, and I had two hours to provide a response. I would then be required to sit in the officials' box in the House of Commons in case of unexpected supplementary questions. It was all a bit surreal, but so exciting.

Towards the end of my time as a civil servant, I was to realise how hazardous this briefing role was. A close colleague, at a Regional Office, was disciplined for providing inaccurate briefing to a Minister about available Intensive Care beds. My colleague had only repeated information provided by a staff nurse, who happened to have answered the Intensive Care Unit phone, but the error was picked up in a parliamentary session by a local MP. My colleague was informed that her error could have led to a vote of no confidence in the government.

This was a powerful reminder of the political significance of our work. When I commenced in post as a civil servant, I naively believed it was my chance to really help improve the health service, but the truth was brought home to me in the civil service induction training.

"Who are you here to serve?" the trainer asked.

"The British public," I confidently replied.

"No, the Ministers," she firmly corrected.

My friends who realised my forte, and lack of hesitation in speaking 'truth to power', were understandably concerned, when I accepted the civil service position, that I would feel repressed and frustrated. What I comfortingly discovered was that within the walls of the civil service, honesty and challenge were usually appreciated, and I was self-confident enough that I did not hesitate to share my thoughts and opinions. It was disappointing, and of course occasionally annoying, when my input was not acted upon but, rather than becoming aggrieved or doggedly labouring a point, as I would have done in my health service roles, this was such a novel environment for me that I surprisingly seemed able to calmly accept rejection of my ideas.

What I also learnt, and amazingly didn't find too hard to comply with, was that outside the confines of the civil service I had to, at all times, appear totally committed to government policy, never expressing a personal view. Speechwriting I enjoyed and, unlike some of my senior colleagues, actually rather admired Ministers who decided to personalise prepared words. What none of us appreciated was an unexpected announcement of a new policy approach. I can remember the surprise when, sitting on the front row of a conference in December 2001, the Secretary of State, with no warning, announced the appointment of 500 Modern Matrons by April 2002. The secret on such occasions was to remain calm, and manipulate any announcement into a positive, sometimes easier said than done. I was on this occasion pleased that my DoH role sat within the Quality not Nursing team.

As part of the quality team, I was asked to be the nurse member of the DoH group establishing the National Institute for Clinical Excellence (NICE). NICE, once up and running, was expected to produce clear guidance for clinicians and to assess new drugs, treatments, and devices for clinical and cost effectiveness. Not only was I the only nurse in the room, but also, until a female psychiatrist joined at a later meeting, the only woman. I know many would be angered by this and would expect me to say that I was treated differently. Maybe I am insensitive, but I can honestly say it never bothered me. I felt that I was treated in the same way as all the other members of the committee. We were all finding our way. What I did come to appreciate in this forum, and indeed when working generally with career civil servants, was how intelligent and focused my colleagues were. The DoH civil service lead, after only a few NICE meetings, had a grasp of chemotherapy worthy of a Consultant Oncologist.

On another project, I was asked to support a young career civil servant who was leading on a review and rewrite of the NHS Consent policies. My role was to facilitate her meeting the 'right' people in the NHS and Medical Royal Colleges. When we first met, and I asked her about her experience with health services, she had no hesitation in informing me that she'd never had contact with the Department of Health. She'd spent the last few years in the House of Commons library. Her only personal health service contact was that she had her tonsils out at age 11.

I approached our first meeting, with a senior surgeon, with trepidation. I was, however, to quickly realise what a good choice she was to lead this work. Without any traditional professional boundaries or experiential baggage, she approached each interview with a freshness that meant she asked questions, and mercilessly probed responses given. The resultant policy and guidance have stood the test of time.

This support role capitalised upon my seniority and thus contacts within the NHS, but within the Department of Health I was certainly considered to be extremely junior and was rarely allowed to come into the presence of Ministers. If I was involved in a meeting attended by a Minister, it was a bit like being a Victorian-era child. I was not expected to speak and often felt invisible, placed in a chair on the periphery of the action. However, as soon as I stepped outside of the civil service environment into the health service, the Department of Health introductory label appeared to give me a free pass for entry anywhere. I'd like to say that it also brought with it respect, but I have to admit it was more likely to promote an atmosphere of wariness, or even fear.

My Northern chattiness usually won through, but I also learnt certain tricks for really getting a feel for a hospital, which in some instances commenced even before entering the NHS premises. On one trip to visit a new hospital in Ireland, my greatest insight came from the loquacious taxi driver taking me from the airport. When I named my destination, he proceeded, with no prompting, to give me a 15-minute lecture on how the new hospital site was smart, but they had made a big mistake.

"They just transferred the crap staff from the old hospitals when they should have sacked the lot of them and started again!" he pronounced.

I shared this public reflection with a rather staggered hospital CEO, and when I asked him to call me a taxi to return to the airport, he eagerly grabbed his car keys to give me a personal lift.

The other tactic that served me well on these visits, capitalising on my generally approachable persona, but also because of my habit of always getting to appointments mega early, was to start a visit with a coffee in the public area café, often a WRVS facility. The volunteer ladies behind the counter were always very happy to chat about how wonderful their hospital was. As tables were often crowded, fellow customers also never hesitated to chatter, telling me with no prompting all about their experiences in the hospital.

On one occasion in 2001, at the newly opened flashy Bristol Children's Hospital, I was joined at my coffee table by a visiting mother of an adolescent. She proceeded to describe to me the limitations of the new build, in terms of room size and adolescent facilities, and even strange curtain rail arrangements.

Unfortunately, or perhaps fortunately, when the CEO an hour later was proudly showing me around, we went on to my coffee companion's son's ward, and, seeing me, she rushed out, greeting me like an old friend. She insisted on showing me, and an embarrassed CEO, exactly what the issues were in her son's cramped room. The designer slanted windows certainly didn't allow for effective curtaining! Seeing beneath the veneer of officially organised and management-controlled hospital visits became my forte. However, although the visits were personally interesting, I debate whether they ever actually had any positive impact on patient care.

Over the three years I visited over 200 UK hospitals. When people now ask me if I've been somewhere in the UK, I can usually say yes but only know the station, hospital, and local basic hotel! My travel arrangements were expertly organised by an excellent secretary. She became far more than just a staff member but my guardian angel and friend. She never went off duty until she knew I was safely installed in my nightly accommodation, and there was only one error in all the visits I made. She booked me to travel and stay in Goole, Yorkshire,

260 miles away from Poole, Dorset, where I was meant to be.

Most of my journeys were by train which gave me many hours for plodding through uninspiring documents. I remember one particularly long journey from Plymouth to Preston. It took 12 hours, due to the UK-wide speed limit temporarily introduced after the Selby train crash in 2001. I boarded the train with a case full of documents and was still working on arrival at Preston.

The DoH post was UK based. It was, therefore, very tempting to accept overseas invitations. I had an enjoyable visit to present the Essence of Care work at the World Health Organisation in Copenhagen. This was my first experience of having to curb my rapid and enthusiastic presentation style so that my speech could be concurrently translated into 10 languages.

The most stressful experience overseas for me was in 2000, before the days of widespread mobile phones. I accepted an invitation to speak at an International Heath Service Management conference in Larissa in Greece. The flight was from Heathrow, and I was aware that there was a problem from the moment I entered the departure lounge. My heart sank when I observed additional temporary seating being laid out. It was then announced that the UK air traffic control system had failed, and only one flight was able to leave at a time. There followed many hours in the airport, and many hours sitting in the plane on the runway, which was where I made my first mistake.

Trying to be helpful, I agreed to swap seats so that my neighbours' friend could move to sit next to her. I did not discover, until it was too late, that the 'friend's' seat was on the back row of the plane, which was a smoking area. After eight hours on the runway in a sealed plane, I was sitting in a smoky fog! Fearing respiratory failure and realising that I would now miss my contact and lift for the four-hour drive from Athens to Larissa, I asked to alight. I was informed that, as the luggage was on board, this was impossible.

We eventually landed in Athens at 2 a.m. (12 hours late), to a virtually closed airport.

Package holiday makers were quickly loaded onto waiting buses, leaving me stranded. I found a leaflet for an Athens hotel, and made my way to a taxi rank, where I handed the driver the leaflet.

My suspicions were aroused when we turned down ever more dingy streets, certainly not a tourist area. When we stopped, the driver hurried me into an unmarked building. He chunnered in Greek to a man behind a desk, and then hurriedly left. There was no obvious reception area, or indeed any sign of communal hotel facilities. The man took my case, and I followed him up two flights of stairs, to be shown into a room that reinforced all my concerns.

The large bed, set under a mirrored ceiling, was made up in red silk sheets. There was a video player with a selection of unlabelled videos, and three Greek nude statues distributed around the room. The man left, and I bolted the door, strategically leaning a statue of Aphrodite against it, so that if anyone entered, she would fall into the mirror-fronted wardrobe doors. The phone rang, and a man asked if he could come and check the room temperature.

"No thanks, I like it hot," was my classic response.

It was now around 3:30 a.m., and sleep was not an option, so I sat on the bed with my portable computer and wrote a ministerial briefing paper that was due in on my return. My disquieting thoughts were, 'no one knows where I am', and 'I need to get to safety'. At 6 a.m. I decided to make my move. Quietly, and with great trepidation, I left the room, descended the stairs, and crept out of the unattended front door. I dragged my suitcase through the back streets of Athens for around an hour, until I found a major road.

I then attempted to hail a taxi, failed, but eventually found a taxi rank. I debated asking for a ride to the station, as I knew trains ran to Larissa, but I had no idea where I was to be staying in Larissa. I dismissed this plan when I was told by the driver that trains were limited as it was Sunday, and Monday was a National holiday. Exhausted and scared, I decided my inconsequential speech would not be missed, and asked to be driven to Athens airport.

Once in the check-in area, I at least felt safe, but the airline staff were totally unhelpful. They told me to just sit on a chair, and they would let me know if a seat on a flight to the UK became available. Much to the annoyance of the check-in staff, after watching two UK flights leave, I stood leaning on their counter whilst every UK passenger checked in for the next 13:30 Heathrow flight. At 13:00, I was dismissively tossed a docket to take to the airline desk to pay for a ticket, to then bring it back to get a boarding pass. I would then need to get through passport control etc.

On arriving at the airline desk there was a long queue, and at this point, scared and exhausted, I burst into tears. A kindly Greek gentleman at the front of the queue asked me what was wrong, and, hearing my story, took control, getting me my ticket. I ran back to the check-in desk, the boarding pass was unceremoniously thrown at me, and with all my luggage, I rushed through passport control and security, and ran to the gate. I arrived in a heap, just as the bridge was being removed. Again, I burst into tears, and the perturbed bridge controller reversed the controls, allowing me to board and collapse sobbing into a seat. Surrounding passengers were unnerved, and as soon as we took off the gentleman next to me, not knowing the problem, demanded the hostess bring me a brandy! I then slept!

Setting foot back in England was such a relief, and even though I then arrived at Euston to find a total signal failure had delayed all trains North, I just felt safe again. I contacted the conference organisers once home, but never had an acknowledgement or further contact from them.

It took many years for me to visit Athens again, and when I did, I was escorted by a Greek colleague. Knowing this story, she was determined to not only show me the beauty of her capital city, but to restore my faith in Athenians, taking me to have a magnificent homecooked dinner with her parents.

This abortive trip was to be my last overseas visit as a civil servant. The excessive UK travel, the exhausting lifestyle, and the resultant lack of any personal life took its toll. I decided that, after three years, time had come to move on. It certainly wasn't because I hated the job. On the contrary; although at times frustrated, I loved it. There was a certain excitement, and definite buzz about working where decisions were made, even though I was rarely involved and certainly was not always in agreement. I actually believe that the professional skills I developed during my time as a civil servant, particularly around preparing briefs and report writing, and the fundamental understanding I developed as to the role of the civil service and Ministers and how the UK is actually run and governed, have been invaluable. I always felt proud when walking down Whitehall, even though our office was hidden in the attic.

CHAPTER 6

HEALTH SERVICE MANAGEMENT

- Service Manager 1992–1993 (Alder Hey Children Hospital, Liverpool)
- Director of Nursing and Workforce Development (Great Ormond Street Hospital, London (GOSH)) 2002–2010

In 1992 I took a management post in the Cardiac and Intensive Care Directorate at Alder Hey Children's Hospital in Liverpool. I started this time as a Service Manager with a bang. In the previous months, the Royal College of Surgeons had been invited to review the practice of one of the hospital's senior female cardiothoracic surgeons. Unhappy with the recommendations, which apparently did not question the excellence of her clinical skills, but her interpersonal and communication style, the surgeon left the country to take up a senior position overseas. Parents were furious as she had instilled in them, either covertly or perhaps overtly, a belief that, due to the complexity of their child's abnormal heart structure, she was the only one who could safely perform any further surgery.

She had left before I started, so we had never met, but on day one in post I was informed by the police that a viable death threat had been made against me as Manager, and that I was to be assigned police protection. It was all totally surreal. For days police checked under my car with mirrors and escorted me to and from work. What an introduction to health service management, but through it all I did have great sympathy for the parents' plight.

I had less sympathy, later in my time as a Service Manager, for the threatening behaviour of nursing staff, experienced by my fellow managers when they had to inform staff that, due to shift changes, a full-time member of the night staff would be required to work an extra shift a month. My colleagues had cars purposefully scratched, lockers kicked in, and some of them were even physically threatened. It came to the evening that I was to face my nursing team. I had got so anxious and worked up that I had a cracking migraine. I knew I had to attend the meeting, so gripping a vomit bowl I entered the room of aggrieved nurses, fearing for my safety. As I entered, an observant sister asked if I was OK, with which I puked into the bowl, and explained I had a migraine. There was an immediate response, with those present reverting from unionised zealots to compassionate nurses. The shift changes went through without a challenge, and I was ushered back to my car with reassurance that I should get to bed and not worry anymore!

This mix of militancy and total commitment and dedication to the children was a recurrent theme as a Manager in Liverpool. The staff were certainly feisty, and it was unlike working anywhere else I had been in my career. I appreciated the staffs' passion and honesty, but bringing about any change, like the move of cardiac services from the dilapidated but beloved Myrtle Street site into the purpose built new cardiac wing at Alder Hey, took consistent positivity and cool perseverance. It was a bit exhausting!

The cardiac staff were very content once relocated, and the Paediatric Intensive Care Unit staff, still located at this time in the old Alder Hey ward blocks, were envious of the truly state-of-the-art unit. The gloating over the better facilities evaporated when a digger, involved in the building of a new ward block, managed to dig through not only the main hospital cable but also the backup generator cable supplying the new Cardiac wing! It was like a scene from 'Mash', with staff in the windowless Cardiac Intensive Care Unit working by torch light to transfer the children onto battery or hand-pumped systems. They were then running them down the main corridor to the antiquated but reliable PICU. The children were all safely transferred. That day I saw the very best of Liverpool nursing.

The commitment and skills of all Alder Hey nurses were undeniable, but I have to admit I have never totally understood the unique Liverpool psyche. Liverpudlians are to me an unexpected disparate mix of the very best of society; generous, fun, and caring, versus aggrieved and sometimes aggressively defensive. On the wards, fights between parents were not rare. I was even called upon to negotiate peaceful resolutions when accusations of minor theft were made. On the other hand, I saw some of the most moving acts of kindness. There was a memorable Christmas Eve when staff on the Paediatric Intensive Care Unit were absolutely furious when a parent's car was broken into, and all the child and siblings' presents stolen. Within an hour, an appeal had gone out on the radio to return the presents, and although the thieves appeared to be unrepentant, generous individuals flooded the hospital with gifts.

An outpouring of caring but aggressive emotion was also evident the awful week of James Bulger's murder in February 1993. I was the Duty Manager when the tortured body of this young boy arrived at the hospital and I witnessed the awful distress of the police, staff, and public that night. The outpouring of emotion was physically visible in the vast number of flowers and stuffed toys that rapidly appeared at the shopping centre where James had been abducted. The police became worried about public order, and asked Alder Hey to accept the offerings at the hospital. What arrived was a truck load of bedraggled flowers and soaking wet teddies, which we rapidly realised could not be salvaged. Having carefully checked that all messages had been retrieved, we, with as much decorum as we could engender in the task, placed the discarded dead flowers and irretrievable soft toys in a skip at the back of the hospital. We had just completed our sad task when the on-call phone rang, and a local paper asked if they could come and take a photo of the soft toys. Two porters spent the following hour in the skip, retrieving soggy teddies for one of the saddest photo shoots I've ever been involved in.

This was one of many sad days I was to witness during my time at Alder Hey, as the staff in my Directorate were caring for some of the sickest children in the North West. I strangely found these deaths, and observing the inconsolable grief of the parents, affected me more than when I had been a ward sister. I could not directly help, but rather reluctantly had to recognise that my role was now to support others, and to facilitate the smooth running of the Unit.

For the first time in my career, I had to rapidly become a business manager, spending hours juggling workforce figures, budgets, commissioning, contracting, and writing business cases. I am a fast learner, and although I rebelled against spending most of my days locked in a paper-filled office, by insisting that I still worked the occasional nursing shift, I quickly grasped what was required from me. My greatest challenge was yet again some of the senior medical team, who strongly objected to being managed. I remember, for example, the horrific behaviour of the senior cardiothoracic surgeon at my first meeting with the specialist commissioners. We were meeting to discuss activity figures and funding, but the surgeon pompously refused to answer any questions or address any concerns raised. He not only seemed to be insensitive to the impact his dismissive approach was having upon the commissioning team, and indeed any future funding, but even seemed to be pleased with his grandstanding approach. Horrified, I desperately retrieved the situation, providing the required figures which I had prepared, and interjecting with the phrase, "What Mr. X is trying to say is …" He was furious, but our contract was saved.

Sadly, this surgeon was the Clinical Lead for the Cardiac Unit, and our relationship never improved, although I don't think he really cared as he deemed me beneath his consideration. Indeed, he regarded any management involvement as totally unnecessary. There was a classic day when I handed him the final draft of the year's business plan, which I had spent ages pulling together, but which he needed to sign off. He rose from his chair, to draw the attention of his medical colleagues, and ripped the paper into shreds, ceremoniously dumping it into the bin.

"This is what I think of Business Planning!" he stated to the audience.

"Good job it can be printed again then," I furiously retorted.

This doctor was apparently a good surgeon in terms of technical ability, but had little compassion for the children and families, or indeed staff. As my sister once said, "You have to be pretty pompous to believe you can put your hands in a child's chest and make a difference."

He should never have been given management responsibilities.

The clinical lead for the Paediatric Intensive Care Unit, the other arm of my Directorate, was the complete opposite. She was not only an excellent and kind intensivist, but also an excellent manager. She was highly supportive and restored my faith in medics as managers, as long as they are the right medics!

The Service Manager post taught me so much that was to be invaluable in my future career, but it was the post I least enjoyed in my working life. The one saving grace for me was that, when I accepted the post, the Directorate had a tripartite management structure, with the Service Manager on a managerial par with the Directorate Clinical Lead, and we all reported to the Hospital Directors. Eighteen months into the post, I was informed that Service Managers were now to directly report to the Clinical Lead. I could not accept reporting to the Cardiac Surgeon, for whom I had no respect. I found a lower paid position in education and resigned.

I was extremely sad to leave and, in a way, felt guilty to abandon some of the excellent colleagues and friends I had made at Liverpool. On my last day, they had organized a 'leaving do' lunch, but this was not to be. At 11 a.m., as I was preparing to close everything down and enjoy my leisurely farewell meal, the phone rang to say that a major incident had been declared. We needed to prepare for a possible influx of children requiring ventilation, following chlorine gas poisoning. I initially thought it was an amusing hoax for my last day, but not so! There had been an undetected fault at a Liverpool swimming pool, and chlorine gas had been pumped into the changing rooms just as a school group were changing. It was all hands-on deck. A ward was cleared, ventilators borrowed from Broad Green Hospital and reset to paediatric settings, and we awaited the arrival of around fifty children. Happily, on arrival and assessment, panic attack breathing difficulties were more in evidence than actual chlorine gas damage, and the incident was closed at 6 p.m., just as I left the hospital for the final time!

My next foray into health service management was in 2002, when I was appointed as the Director of Nursing and Workforce Development at Great Ormond Street Children's Hospital, London. Perhaps the most sought-after paediatric nursing management post in the country, it was a complex remit as my responsibilities also included human resource management and the educational development of all staff.

I was, within days, to recognise some of the challenges I may face in this coveted position. On day four it was the annual open Board meeting. At the time a very distressed family, whose baby with an untreatable brain deformity had been refused admission to the hospital, was pillaring the hospital, and seriously threatening various staff members and their families. The courts were involved, and various injunctions were in place to protect the staff. However, there was still great concern about staff safety and, before the Board meeting was due to start, the police arrived with bullet-proof vests for Board members. We refused them, and the meeting went without a hitch, but it certainly added to the drama of my first ever NHS Board meeting.

The second day was a totally different clue to my life ahead. Princess Anne was to visit the HIV unit, and I was to sit next to her at lunch. She opened the conversation with, "How many beds does the hospital have?"

"A lot," was my hopeless response.

"And how many children with HIV do you treat?" she asked.

"Quite a few," was my pathetic response.

She soon realised that the Director of Nursing knew nothing, and determinedly turned to her other neighbour. I concentrated on politely eating my lunch.

Royal visits were a regular occurrence at GOSH, and I had learnt my lesson.

Questions were never as badly answered again. I became an expert at preparing for, and planning Royal events, including organising a unique Royal outing in 2004.

Princess Diana had been a regular visitor to GOSH, and in July

2004 we received an invite to attend the opening of the Diana memorial fountain. I decided to take with me a Consultant Child Psychiatrist, who had been involved in a community project funded by Diana's charity, a bereavement care sister from PICU, and a black health care assistant, Jean. Jean worked in the operating theatres and had looked after Diana in 1995 when she observed an operation at the hospital. The three of them had never met royalty before, and, having donned our best 'bib and tucker', we arrived with great excitement at the security check point in Hyde Park.

Security was incredibly tight as the whole Royal family, and the Spencer family, were to be present. We quickly realised how lucky we had been to be invited, as it was a small select event with only representatives of the charities Diana had supported. A marquee had been erected in the middle of a large fenced off area, which was surrounded by an eager public. On entering the marquee, we were offered a glass of champagne and, dry mouthed from excitement, and indeed the heat of the day, three of us eagerly accepted. Jean hesitated as she had never had alcohol. Very foolishly we encouraged her to partake because this was such a special occasion. When we next looked, she had downed the glass in one and was on a second offering. Jean was less keen on the skimpy caviar-based canapes. It soon became obvious that the alcohol had certainly relaxed her into losing any inhibitions.

As the Royal family mingled, I watched with horror, but I must admit with some amusement, as Jean threw her arms around Prince Harry, explaining in an eager tone how she had loved their mother, and how she had looked after her in the GOSH operating theatres. He was polite but looked a little staggered to find himself being bear hugged. It was the with a certain amount of dread that I saw the Queen and Prince Philip approaching, but although Jean was effusive the Queen was correctly greeted by us all. Our psychiatry colleague even managed to remain polite when Prince Philip decided to instruct her on how to handle 'disturbed children with firm discipline'.

The whole atmosphere of the event was tense, and the Spencer family were in a way more difficult to interact with, partly as they tried too hard to be 'matey', which just didn't work. For example, Diana's sister commented to the PICU sister,

"Don't you wish you could go outside for a fag?"

"No, I don't smoke. It's very bad for you," the nurse calmly responded.

I found the whole event intense and exhausting, and just longed to leave, but, as with every Royal event, the Royal family had to leave first. In an attempt to escape the formalities, and indeed to sober up Jean, as soon as permitted we decided to walk around the fountain perimeter. This was my favourite moment, with Jean gaily waving at the barrier crowds.

"Hi, it's me, Jean," she repeatedly shouted.

She was thoroughly enjoying every moment of this unique experience. I, in a way, envied her unreserved approach, perhaps emphasized by alcohol, but I think more about her natural open character.

My most challenging experience of working with Royalty was

during a trip to our GOSH Office in Dubai. We were asked to help facilitate a visit by Prince Andrew, in his role as UK Trade Ambassador. The most senior and influential health leaders in Dubai gathered at the allotted time at the Health City reception area, and we all expectantly awaited the arrival of the Prince. Thirty minutes later there was still no sign. We then received a message that he was tired so would be two hours late. As a UK representative it was incredibly embarrassing, and I found myself effusively apologizing. By the time he swanned in, with no words of apology, I was furious. I couldn't resist a sarcastic comment about the joys of waiting for someone whilst they had a rest. I should not have wasted my time, as Prince Andrew obviously considered it totally appropriate that all arrangements, however inconvenient to others, should be focused on his welfare. He further lost any respect I may have had for him when, that evening, he only made a fleeting appearance at the evening trade reception, being held in his honour at the British Embassy, because he was apparently off to play golf with a friend in Abu Dhabi.

Life at GOSH was certainly never dull and, as well as momentous Royal visits, on a day-to-day basis we encountered the visiting rich and famous, and some more unusual visitors. On returning to my office one routine day, having gone to collect a coffee, my secretary asked, "Anything going on in reception?"

"Not really – just two gnomes, a fairy, and a unicorn," was my disinterested reply. A normal GOSH day.

My favourite risk assessment for a visit was when the cardiac surgeons decided, for research purposes, to MRI scan a live crocodile from London Zoo. It could not be sedated so that its heart function was not affected, and, as due to the magnet there could be no metal in the room, guns were banned. There were a few anxious moments, but all went well, and the next week in the press Peter Pan's Crocodile hit the press.

Fundraising was also a requirement of my role, as the excellence of GOSH was, and indeed is, reliant on the incredible generosity of supporters. It was not a role I enjoyed as I hated asking anyone for money, and I'm certainly not good at putting up with prima donna behaviour. The GOSH charity team were superb, reassuring me that my role was to be passionate about the needs of the children, GOSH, and the care we provided, leaving any 'asking' up to them.

For large fundraising events they presented us with a briefing folder with vital details about all who were going to be present. On one particularly embarrassing evening in early 2008, I had been so busy all day that I had failed to even open the vital folder.

Circulating and checking out Formula One items that were to be auctioned, I was approached by a small, mixed race young man.

"What do you do?" he asked me.

I replied, explaining my role at GOSH, and then asked, "And what do you do?"

I could not understand why my very reasonable return question was met with gasps by those around, and a scandalized look from his companion.

"I drive very fast," he calmly replied.

This was an understatement from Lewis Hamilton! Unimpressed,

I dug an even deeper hole when, listening in to his telling a questioner he had just moved to Switzerland for greater anonymity, I said,

"You should have moved near me as I had no idea who you were." Not my best fundraising moment!

Great Ormond Street Hospital is world famous, and although during my time as Director of Nursing I presented at many UK and International conferences, being invited to represent GOSH at non-nursing international events was an honour that only occasionally came my way.

A memorable outing for the CEO and myself was to Dublin, at the invitation of the Éire government who were in the throes of building a new children's hospital. Expecting our one-night stay to be in the usual nice, but reasonable, NHS-style accommodation, we were rather staggered when, on arriving at Dublin airport, we were ushered into a sleek government car, smoothly passed through a Garda check point, and arrived at the most amazing stately home in the middle of Phoenix Park. As guests of the government, we were to spend the night at Farmleigh, the official Irish state guest house, formerly one of the Dublin residences of the Guinness family. The previous month's guest had been Kofi Anan, seventh Secretary-General of the United Nations.

I was ill-prepared for the formality of our trip, as that evening included a formal dinner, which, as the only residents at Farmleigh, we were hosting. I only had my one business suit and two very sombre professional blouses. I felt very dowdy as the eager guests, many of whom had never been allowed in Farmleigh before, arrived in their glad rags! As always in Ireland the company was excellent and the alcohol flowed. The most surreal moment was standing under the stone pillared entrance of this magnificent house, waving farewell to our guests as though we owned the place.

The staff, our staff, were highly attendant and the next morning, when we had free time, encouraged us to wander the 78-acre private deer park before a private visit to see the Book of Kells at Trinity College. We felt like royalty when the tourists were required to wait in an ever-lengthening queue, whilst these two unknowns enjoyed their leisurely private tour. Embarrassing, but not as embarrassing as that afternoon when, on our return from a meeting at the Hospital, I was, at the suggestion of the staff, relaxing in the magnificent Farmleigh library.

I was curled up on the leather sofa, just checking my speech for a conference to be held in Farmleigh's conservatory later that day, when the door burst open. In came a lady with a red rope, which she clipped onto hooks to prevent entry further than three feet into the room. She then ushered four ladies into the roped entrance area and started describing the fascinating history of the Benjamin Iveagh Library. She proudly stated that this splendid collection contained more than 5,000 items, spanning 800 years of Irish life, and included first editions of Ulysses and Gulliver's Travels. No reference was made to the strange lady sitting statue still on the sofa. Having completed her explanation, the ladies were ushered out and the rope unclipped. Once I had recovered, I felt honoured to be able to privately and very carefully explore this incredible room and its contents. The conference went well, and the CEO and I got the evening flight back to reality, and London public transport home!

Another particularly memorable conference was when the CEO asked me to represent GOSH at a three-day conference in Porto, Portugal. Plans were being finalised for the building of a much-needed Children's Hospital in Porto, and my remit was to emphasise the clinical and research advantages of having a Children's Hospital. I set off with enthusiasm, expecting three days of fun and sun in a beautiful place. Things went wrong from day one.

I was due to speak after a Government official who was expected to announce funding and progress with the exciting Porto Children's Hospital plans. As the conference started the all-too-obvious dawned on me, that the whole event was to be in Portuguese, tricky when your only knowledge of Portuguese is one word, 'obrigado'.

Even though I did not understand a word of the official's opening speech, it did not take Einstein to realise that something was amiss when delegates started throwing missiles, including tomatoes, at him. I must have looked panicked, wondering if I was to suffer a similar fate, and my kindly neighbour on the stage top table leant across and patted my arm.

"You will be fine," he said, but alarmed me further by explaining, "this official has just told us funding has been pulled and the plans for a children's hospital are cancelled."

My speech, based on why plans should have gone ahead, must have been like salt in the wound, but I escaped unscathed.

Then came the decision about what to do for the next three days, as it seemed pointless to sit through lectures when I couldn't understand a word. I decided to explore Porto, which was again rather disastrous as it never stopped raining. It was a very lonely three days, sitting sheltering in café's, but I became a real fan of the Portuguese approach to the drinking of Port before, with, and after every meal!

My GOSH management responsibilities certainly led to numerous meetings and drowning in emails, but I was determined as a Director to maintain my nursing roots, to never fear walking onto a ward, and to be seen and known by as many staff as possible. During my eight years I had a rota in my diary to make sure that each month I visited every ward and department. These walk around visits were of limited value as, as soon as I was seen, staff became so amazingly busy that it was inappropriate to interrupt them, and parents seemed to pick up their reluctance to speak to this suited stranger.

A truly back to the floor approach was needed. Therefore, as often as I was able, I donned a staff nurse's uniform, appropriate for my level of clinical competence, and joined the hospital-wide clinical site practitioner team. This was usually for part of a night shift, as this limited management interruptions. This arrangement seemed to make staff and parents more relaxed about chatting to me, but the nurses, due to the very effective hospital grapevine, never seemed surprised to see me.

I was impressed and humbled by what I saw, and in a way this exposure to the frontline was more of a motivator for me than the staff, who seemed happy in their work. This shift work did allow me to observe true interactions between staff. I was so relieved that, in the main, there appeared to be mutual respect between the medical and nursing teams. The only time I had to pick up on poor behaviour from a junior doctor was when I volunteered to help the catering staff serve lunch in the canteen. The doctor started shouting the odds over the amount he was being asked to pay for chips! I had great delight in revealing my position and an apology was immediately offered to the upset cashier.

When I started at GOSH, I primarily saw my role as leading the >3,000 nurses, but the truth was that I had an excellent Deputy, and four Assistants, who had the nursing function well under control. Most of my time was taken up with my role as Director of Workforce Development, which included the Director of HR function. I had no formal HR qualification, just practical expertise gained in managing staff and a lot of common sense. This could have endangered GOSH, but I knew my limitations, and was fearful enough to always seek help and advice from the experts. I was knowledgably guided and supported by the Head of HR and his team. They patiently taught me so much about HR policies, procedures, and employment law, and together I believe we made GOSH a great place to work.

Over my time at GOSH, the team certainly faced some hard times, and my inner strength and skills as a leader were put to the test. Having been in post for three years, it was on July 7th, 2005, that I came to truly appreciate that, even if on a day-to-day basis staff constantly challenge leaders' decisions, in times of unbelievable crisis, staff, at every level, will turn to their leaders to LEAD. It was a usual Thursday morning Board meeting, but I had to leave early for a meeting at the Regional Headquarters on Tottenham Court Road. I set off for a pleasant walk, taking my usual route through Russell Square.

Whilst chattering to my friend Kathy on my mobile phone, there was suddenly, at 09:47, an enormous bang. Without hesitation I calmly said to my staggered friend,

"Sorry I'll have to go. A bomb has just gone off."

I was unaware of the mayhem now unfolding only yards away in Tavistock Square where the bus bomb had killed 13 people. I hurried back to GOSH, oblivious at this point that at 8:49 three bombs had been detonated on underground tubes, and beneath us people were dying in the Russell Square tube tunnel.

I will be forever sad that, on that day, we lost two of our loyal staff, a young nurse lost a limb and many staff required long-term psychological support. However, what I will also remember with incredible pride is how GOSH staff reacted. Within minutes we realised that we were the nearest hospital to the Russell Square tube bomb site, and due to the Tavistock Square bomb, ambulances could not get through security roadblocks. The hospital canteen was immediately cleared and transformed into a major incident triage centre. Staff members went underground to take vital drugs and medical equipment, and to sit with the injured and dying. I still shudder when I see press pictures of our staff running down Guilford Street with stretchers. The efforts of GOSH staff were recognised in the London Assembly report on the incident, published in June 2006. It stated, 'Great Ormond Street Hospital played a crucial role in the rescue and treatment of the injured at Russell Square, even setting up a field hospital'.

All staff desperately wanted to help, and in a way the day was easier for those directly involved. Indeed, many of the staff with longer term psychological care needs were not on the frontline that day. Most staff had to continue routine care of the children in the hospital. It has always impressed me that, even in the midst of this carnage, the cardiothoracic team managed to perform a heart transplant, determined not to lose the matching organ.

I had always been described as 'good in a crisis', but this day there were moments of such personal doubt. As soon as I had returned to the hospital, the major incident plan was activated. My primary role was the deployment of staff to where they were most needed. The instruction in a crisis was that all 'spare' staff should report to the Board Room. This was a fully staffed Thursday morning, and I entered to a room crammed with over 200 noisy staff. As I entered silence fell, and all faces turned to me with a look of desperate expectation. I froze. Next to me, a Consultant Radiologist calmly pulled across a chair, took my hand, and guided me to stand on it so as to be visible to all.

"Judith, we all trust you. Tell us what we need to do," she quietly whispered.

I have never felt so responsible for the welfare of so many, so respected but also so motherly. The rest of the day passed in a blur of activity, all aimed at keeping everyone safe. GOSH became a safe island amidst mayhem. Because of police lockdown, communication from outside was reliant on emerging news broadcasts and my regular foray to the silver command barrier on Tavistock Square.

Nobody was allowed to leave, which meant that, in addition to inpatients and their families, a vast number of children and families, who had arrived for outpatient appointments and same day treatment, had to also be safely cared for. Local Italian restaurants arrived with enormous pans of pasta dishes, and children's entertainment was organized. Parents were less easily distracted and were just desperate to leave, which meant policing the exits, and each hour a senior nurse climbed on a chair in reception and provided an update, often with nothing new to say.

I spent the next 48 hours constantly on the move, calming and reassuring. I checked if staff were safe and had managed to contact and reassure their own families. The horrific moment was realising some staff had not arrived on shift. Liaising with their distraught families, desperate efforts were made to try and locate them. The death of the two murdered staff members was not confirmed for around two weeks.

Whilst busy, my own emotions around the bombing were held in check. I realised at four p.m. that, midst this frenetic activity, I had forgotten to reassure my own family. Having phoned my sister, I rang my parents who were already in the first stages of dementia and living in their own bubble of reality. I had a surreal conversation about the price and availability of chunky marmalade.

My other major personal concern that day was that my Australian friends, and their two young sons, were arriving that morning to stay with me in the Barbican. They could tell their own story of arriving at Paddington in the midst of the 9.00 mayhem. On the instruction of the police, they walked with large cases and two terrified children, the four and a half miles from Paddington to my flat. I managed, with relief, to contact them once they reached the safety of the flat, and there they stayed until I could get home on Friday evening. The youngest son retreated to lying under my dining room table, and it was a few days before we could tempt him out with a trip to Hamley's toy shop, although riding a bus took a lot more effort and bribery.

I held my emotions together until the moment of the Europe-wide two-minute silence on July 14th. I was that morning staying up North with my friend Kathy, and I decided we would go and sit in the local church for our two minutes silence. Sitting in a pew, I became aware that we were alone in our observance of the silence. There was no pause in external activity, or even in the activity around the church. I started unconsolably sobbing, and once I started, I could not stop.

"They don't care, why don't they care?" I blurted out to Kathy between sobs.

Despite Kathy's stoic efforts to reassure and calm, for the first time in my life I just longed to be back in London with others who would truly understand.

Although the most challenging day, the July 2005 bombing was not to be the only major incident during my eight years at GOSH. I was, for example, to become an expert on the explosive nature of blocked sewage stacks, the danger of unsafe ceiling-mounted televisions, and how to limit the impact of massive re-building projects on activity. Through it all the staff were superb, calm, and professional. This was particularly demonstrated in September 2008, when staff rapidly and safely evacuated all the children from the cardiac wing, when a faulty TV caused a major fire. I still remember the disbelief, and indeed relief we all felt, when watching security camera footage from that day. It showed a critically sick child on life-saving equipment being run out of the ward door by a fireman and nurses, ten seconds before the ward cylinders exploded, blowing out the door and external wall.

Life was never quiet as an NHS Trust Director, and even when not on call the phone rang night and day. It was certainly a full-time job. One night is always remembered by my niece, who was living in the Barbican flat with me at the time. Helen had been out with friends and got home at midnight. After quietly making herself a cup of tea in the magnolia- coloured kitchen she went to bed. At 3 a.m. my on-call phone rang. The police wanted permission to let dogs off in the basement of the hospital, as there were intruders who had let off some of the fire extinguishers. Having checked all children were safely behind locked ward doors, I agreed, and asked to be informed once all was safely resolved. Unable to return to bed until assured all was well, I decided to paint the kitchen walls with the bright orange paint I had purchased but had never got around to using. At 5 a.m., painting completed, and having been given the 'all clear' by the police, I returned to bed. At 7 a.m. Helen, having got up for work, burst into my room, saying something strange had happened overnight!

Most of my out-of-hours calls were related to child protection issues, which I tended to receive even when I was not on call, as they were usually complex and outside the comfort zone of the nonclinical Directors. Although, after 20 years in paediatrics, and having undertaken copious amounts of child protection training, I was able to support and guide others; I was not the official GOSH safeguarding lead until February 2008. I was asked to accept this addition to my role in response to the Baby P furore.

Peter had been murdered on August 3rd, 2007, but it was only on publication of the coroner's report in 2008 that GOSH realised that a GOSH-employed community paediatrician had failed to examine Peter on August 1st. There followed years of intense activity, which I can only reflect on as being the most personally challenging of my career. Because North Middlesex Hospital Paediatric Services were in 2007 managed by GOSH, I was actually in A&E with the Paediatric Matron when Peter's tortured little body was brought in. I will never forget the sight and the intense sadness we all felt.

What followed was professionally lifechanging. I had never before experienced such manipulation of facts in order to pass the buck between professionals, and the intense search for someone to blame. Yes, mistakes were made by many professionals, and it was the most horrific outcome, but I can still 'hand on heart' say that, as far as I was concerned, GOSH made every attempt to be as forthright as the lawyers would allow. When, at the instruction of a Senior Barrister (a QC), documents were redacted to protect other children, including Peter's siblings, we were pilloried for hiding the truth, and this personally, and professionally, hurt.

All were quick to point the finger at the HVs, SWs, and the community paediatrician, and the pressure was so great that some professionals never practiced again, and all involved had to be offered counselling. There is no denying that everyone involved knew that they had, for a variety of reasons, failed to protect Peter. We acknowledged and apologised for where we had gone wrong, but the basic truth that I tried to consistently get across to staff was that they did not actually kill Peter. They were just made to feel they had. Indeed, the frontline press were a nightmare, relentlessly contacting staff, and even forcing their way into the home of a seriously ill staff member, until thankfully stopped by the press complaints commission. I was glad I lived in the very secure Barbican.

At the height of press interest, GOSH was receiving around 200 press queries a day, which necessitated a meeting each afternoon between myself, the GOSH legal lead, and senior comms officer. In addition, there were continuous meetings to attend, reviews to input into, and reports to write, which all involved numerous repetitive questions being asked and answered. It was like feeding an enormous beast when I desperately wanted to be able to concentrate time and effort on learning from this sad event, to try and make sure it never happened again.

What I did learn through this time was the vital importance of visible senior management, in supporting staff to not only cope but survive the incredible pressure and feelings of guilt that follow such a horrific incident. Although the community paediatricians in Haringey were being managed by GOSH at the time of Peter's death, GOSH only took over the management of the whole of Haringey Community Children's Services in April 2008, nine months after Peter's death. Haringey staff were still floundering. Case load numbers, which had been abysmal when Peter died, were getting even worse as new staff hesitated to join. The team were exhausted and disillusioned, but they remained amazingly loyal to each other and the families in their care.

On the advice of a friend, who had turned around paediatric services in Grantham after the Beverley Allitt serial killer case, I decided to base myself for three days a week in Haringey. This not only allowed me to face-to-face support the Haringey team, but to also work with them in reviewing all policies and procedures. Together we took a deep breath and positively moved forward. The service started to recover, and these six months transformed my own commitment to keeping children healthy. I felt embarrassed about how, as an acute hospital paediatric nurse, I had previously dismissed the importance of the work of my health visiting colleagues. I was a convert!

It is easy now to reflect on how the Baby P case, and the actions I had to take, positively changed me as a person, but I cannot underestimate how hard it was at the time. People I had respected for years avoided me, others rang daily to check I was OK. My personal friends and my Northern family were the greatest support. They had limited interest in, or understanding of, the case. They just wanted to know that I was OK. When press interest was starting to wane, I had a week's holiday in Sorrento with two friends. They had the sense to allow me to go, each morning, to the Foreigners Club to browse the English newspapers for mention of the case, before banning for the day any further mention of Baby P.

The deal I made myself was that I would not move on from GOSH until the furore had died down. I thought all had calmed down in 2010, when I finally left GOSH. However, this was not to be the case. My picture and name appeared yet again in a Baby P article in the 'Times' in 2012, and even when I applied for the CEO's post at the RCPCH in 2016 I was asked if there would be any reputational risk to the organisation because of the Baby P case. To the contrary, I believe living through, and professionally surviving, the intense media and personal pressure of the Baby P case made me a far better Executive Manager. I emerged from this intense time knowing how to work with the press, even more committed to being open and honest, and able to maintain personal integrity, even when under the most extreme pressure.

Sadly, I also emerged more disillusioned about the behaviour of Ministers and health service leaders at Regional and National level. When they should have been supporting us to improve practice, they had jumped on this incident as self-motivated shroud wavers, very willing to protect themselves by pushing any blame they could on to others.

Over the last year at GOSH my disillusionment with the health service increased. I seemed to be more and more involved in inspections, monitoring, and data collection and less and less in service quality and improvement. GOSH was a great hospital, and in my eight years I received no complaints directly related to nursing care, and yet I was drowning under monitoring every aspect of our service, with some data meaningless given the specialist nature of our work. The final straw came, as it often does in a seemingly inconsequential event, when I was told our star rating would be affected because I had failed to gather data regarding single-sex ward accommodation on every GOSH ward. As far as I was concerned, neonates do not care if their next-door neighbour is of the opposite sex, but to get any exemption from data-gathering requirements took unreasonable effort.

After eight years I also realised I was becoming the sort of miserable soothsayer I had always despised. When I heard myself repeatedly saying to the young and enthusiastic new Chief Operating Officer, 'I can tell you it won't work,' I knew, for GOSH's sake, time had come for me to hand over the reins of this place I loved, and I needed the personal motivation of a new challenge.

Judith at 9 months, 1960

Mum and Dad

Jane, Carol, Helen, Joy, David, 2014

St Thomas's Hospital, 1978

Receiving my Nightingale badge, 1982

Nightingale friends' reunion, 2014

Locky, Andrea, Rory, Kathy, Me, Martin – Australia, 1998

Proud of others children - Carol, Hannah, Amy, Helen, Joy.
Celebrating my OBE 2020

Frances, Liz, Mona, Me, Lynn, Lesley
Kathy, Gail, Kathy, Yolanda, Mary, Cath
60th birthday, January 1st 2020

Leaving Wythenshawe Hospital, 1982

Sydney Hamburger Award, 1984

Paediatric Ward Sister, 1983 -1990

Sunday Custard Pie Fight

Me and Angela (PGCE), 1991

Joy, Me, Carol - PhD day, 2004

Me, Warren, Mary, Nicola: LSBU team

Honorary Doctorate, Oxford Brookes University, 2016

Nightingale NW Hospital, 2020

Frances and me, Lourdes pilgrimage, 1988

Janice, Liz, me, Kathy Shan, Myanmar, 2017

MASCOT

Louise (THET), Marcus & Jenny (H4HC), Ben (THET)

Lesson planning in Somaliland

CHAPTER 7

REGULATION

- Nursing and Midwifery Council (NMC) Member 2009–2014 (interim Chair 2012)
- Family Liaison Team Lead 2020 (Nightingale Covid Hospital, Manchester)

Award:

2020 – Nightingale North West Hospital Star Award

As I have grappled with how the profession I feel so passionate about can really move forward, I have increasingly recognised the difficulty of the wide use of the word 'nurse'. Anyone can call themselves a nurse. We all 'nurse' family members when ill. So how do the public know that this 'nurse' is adequately trained, knows how they are expected to behave and practice, and can be stopped from practicing if they are unsafe?

It is unwieldy to describe yourself as a 'registered nurse', but I cannot see another way around signifying to the public that your practice is regulated, that they are safe in your hands. The importance of regulation was confirmed for me when a friend told me that a new 'nurse' had started at her aunt's care home. I recognised the name and was concerned that, although calling herself a nurse and wearing a uniform, this lady was in fact a care assistant who had left my parents' care home when accused of hitting a resident.

Unregistered, she was able to move and get a new job with vulnerable people.

In 2009, my belief in nursing as a profession, and the need for public protection through registration and regulation, led me to become a Council member of the Nursing and Midwifery Council, the regulator for over 670,000 UK nurses and midwives. It was a total eye opener. A complex organization, whose public protection functions frontline nurses did not, and still do not understand, and which constantly gets confused with the role of the Royal College of Nursing, the union. It is an organisation which is doomed not to please anyone. Nurses object to having to pay the annual fee in order to practice, and the public often disagree with decisions made when a nurse is referred for poor practice.

Indeed, within months of my appointment, I was staggered to receive, whilst on holiday on the Isle of Capri, a phone call from the UK police warning me, as an NMC council member, of a death threat from supporters of Margaret Haywood. This nurse had been removed from the register for video recording poor care, apparently without the permission of the patient.

I doubted any assassin would track me to Capri, but I was a little unnerved as I had not appreciated that serving on the Council would make me the subject of such threats. Over the next five years, I never again received a death threat, but was regularly verbally attacked during conference presentations and received many aggressive emails.

What I came to appreciate and admire was the calm tolerance exhibited by the NMC staff. I was, for example, amused and impressed when, shortly after my return from Capri, the acting CEO, on hearing that a group of elderly ladies with 'Reinstate Margaret' placards were marching up and down in the pouring rain outside NMC headquarters, invited them in to join us for tea and lemon drizzle cake. She listened and they were immediately calmed. Ms Haywood was later reinstated.

The most turbulent times at the NMC came in 2012 with the publication of a very negative report from the Council for Health Regulatory Excellence (CHRE). This coincided with the unexpected resignation of the CEO, and shortly after the Chair, leading to my being asked by other Council members, and the Department of Health regulation team, to stand in as acting Chair for six months.

As acting Chair, the priority was to sort out the fitness to practice activity, which was being overwhelmed with referrals, so that processes and subsequent action was unacceptably protracted.

It became evident that during initial screening, over 35% of received cases were inappropriate. Many of these were public complaints against people using the title 'nurse' who were not actually registered nurses. Other cases received should have been dealt with locally by NHS employers HR departments. This really annoyed me, as by the time an anxious registrant was informed the referral had been closed, they could have suffered months of unnecessary stress.

If a case was deemed worthy of further action, it could be over four years before the case was actually heard, or even longer if there were associated criminal charges. During all this time a nurse may have been prevented from working.

More NMC capacity was required, and this meant more money was needed, which had to come from increasing registrant fees. The profession was not happy. This discontent became only too real for me when a group of six aggrieved registrants, in evening dresses, surrounded and berated me in the ladies' restroom, during a nursing award evening event.

The politicians also waded in, eager to appear loyal to nurses, probably as an election was approaching. One extremely difficult summons, to me and the acting CEO, came from a Health Minister. Sadly, we had decided to meet at an Italian restaurant the night before to make sure we were on message. We ate crab linguine, which was nice at the time, but not when seen again throughout the night. We arrived at Richmond House at Whitehall feeling very rough and were shown into a room where we were left for 40 minutes. Nerves increasing, much to the amusement of the CEO, I decided a quick chorus of 'Always Look on the Bright Side of Life' may be appropriate!

When we were eventually called into a large room, sitting around the table with the Minister were numerous civil servants, and the Chair and CEO of the CHRE. The Minister, herself a former nurse, waded into a tirade as to why the NMC must not, and she said could not, raise the nurses' registration fees. We politely listened to her vitriolic attack, which was accompanied by shouting, pointing, and table slamming. If anyone else tried to speak she immediately silenced them. Unfortunately for her, as a seasoned former civil servant, now employed by the University sector, and as a previous paediatric ward sister used to dealing with tantrummy adolescents, I was unmoved. I knew we had no choice and was very clear that as an independent regulator it was our decision. When she seemed to have run out of steam, I calmly responded,

"I am sorry, Minister, but on April 1st the fees will be increasing,"

She gave the table one more bang, and spluttering a final expletive, stormed from the room. The Chair of the CHRE, whose efforts to intercede had been thwarted, immediately rushed to my side and asked if we were OK, which apart from crab linguine twinges, we certainly were.

The government interference did not stop there. The Secretary of State (SoS) then waded in, accusing the NMC of not adequately calculating the fee rise needed.

Unfortunately, the accusatory letter addressed to me as Chair was released to, and appeared in, the press before it had actually been sent to me. I was furious and drafted an immediate complaint letter to the SoS. The civil servants, who were probably at fault for the premature leaking of the letter to the press, pleaded with me not to send a complaint. I would have been more sympathetic to their appeal, having been a civil servant myself, if it had not come with a veiled threat about challenging a SoS when I was a health professional.

I factually pointed out to them that I was the Dean of a University and Chair of an independent regulator. The SoS, therefore, didn't employ me, he didn't control me, I didn't like or respect him, and didn't even vote for his party. My letter was sent, factually pointing out that his letter was totally inaccurate as we had had two independent reviews of financial requirements and demanding an apology for the premature press release. An apology was forthcoming, but my lowly status was reinforced when in the following weeks I was twice, at short notice, summoned to Whitehall.

Both summonses clashed with the only tickets I had for the London Olympics, still a bone of contention with my family who had travelled from the North so we could all go together to the events! A lifetime opportunity missed, but NMC fees went up and over the next few months, due to the superb effort of the acting CEO and staff team, Fitness to Practice activity was transformed.

The CEO's post was made substantive as my six months as Interim Chair came to an end. I had enjoyed the challenge but, due to employment restrictions, I was not allowed to apply for the substantive position, and a new Chair was appointed. The government again interfered, dictating who was to be put into post. This initially annoyed me as I thought the position should go to open competition and not be government influenced, but their choice was excellent. The new Chair was a true gentleman, and under his leadership a new Council were appointed. I was asked to apply so that I could provide some vital continuity. I was rather half-hearted about staying, and certainly did not approach the recruitment process with vigour.

I was asked to complete psychometric testing on the morning before I was to go teaching in Uganda. I decided to go into the

University early to access the test. I logged in, and the completion time clock started counting down in the corner of the screen. Suddenly, one of the admin staff burst into my office in floods of tears. Her partner had that morning unexpectedly walked out, taking the dog with him. My attempts to calm her took some time, and meanwhile the psychometric clock ran on, until I realised, I now had five minutes to complete a 40-minute test. I just chose random response letters without reading the questions and submitted the test. The day of the interview arrived, and the initial session was a feedback session to share the results of the psychometric test. I was congratulated on how strong my responses had been, responses to questions I hadn't even read! I was offered a seat on the new Council.

Council members had no direct role in Fitness to Practice cases, but in 2013 a case was referred to the NMC that was to lead to international travel for me and Ali, the head of regulation. Victorino Chua, a nurse initially registered in the Philippines, had been arrested in Stockport, UK, charged with poisoning dozens of patients with insulin in 2011 and 2012. He was finally jailed in 2015, but what his case highlighted was the need to review and assure processes for the UK registration of nurses who had initially trained and registered overseas. The police investigating Chua's case could not substantiate that he had ever completed training in the Philippines, and they were worried that he may have purchased fraudulent Filipino registration documentation. This was a great concern for the NMC as at the time there were 32,000 Philippines-trained nurses working in the UK NHS.

I was, unlike Ali, a seasoned traveller, but our trip to the Philippines was a surreal experience. The first barrier was gaining permission for the visit from the Philippines, as the country's economy is heavily dependent on the earnings of professional diaspora working in wealthy nations. At an uncomfortable meeting at the Philippines Embassy in London, accompanied by representatives from the UK Home Office, and Foreign and Commonwealth Office, we were quizzed as to what we hoped to achieve in our proposed visit. In the broadest terms it was not a difficult question. We just wanted to be assured that the UK public were being safely cared for by nurses who had been appropriately trained.

No decision was communicated to us by the embassy, but we were told by the Home Office to book our flights as the situation needed rapid resolution. I have never felt so out of my depth! Still awaiting permission, flights were booked, and on the day of travel, Ali and I set off to Heathrow still unsure if we were to be allowed into the Philippines. We asked again before check in. The answer: "no decision yet but check in and ring before boarding." We rang before boarding; "no decision yet but board and ring when you reach Hong Kong." We rang at Hong Kong; "no definitive decision but fly to Manila and the British Embassy staff will be there to meet you."

Sure enough, Colin, a very pleasant, very tattooed, senior embassy official in jeans was there to greet us. He whisked us to the Embassy secure compound, where we were given the good news that we were now allowed to check in to a Manila Hotel.

The next day Colin, now transformed to senior status in a pristine suit with no tattoos showing, respectfully escorted us to a series of meetings. Luckily the first was to meet the nurse education team at Manila University, where, because of my nursing and University background, we developed an immediate rapport. They freely chattered and vitally explained the history of nurse education in the Philippines, including important changes that had been introduced in 2002.

The relaxed discussion continued on an informal tour of Manila General Hospital. Due to my charity work in Africa, I was used to the traumatic sights within low-resource hospital settings. Leaving a squeamish Ali and Colin, and the government shadow we had now gained, at the door, I was fascinated by all I was shown. For example, Continuous Positive Airway Pressure ventilation of babies being delivered using empty mayonnaise bottles and crammed maternity wards with three mothers per bed pushing out their new- borns.

There followed a series of small meetings with various nursing colleges, and then came the formal briefing meeting organised by the Philippines Government. A nightmare! The three of us entered a large room to find a ten-chair three-sided square, four chairs deep, and in the middle, there were three chairs for 'the accused' – us! This was a moment for me to find my 'good in a crisis' persona. I calmly led the way to the chairs, smiling and greeting all, even though an awkward silence had fallen on the room as we'd entered. The colleagues I had already met, who looked incredibly embarrassed, eagerly returned my smile and greeting.

Before we had even introduced ourselves, our Philippines

government minder leapt from her chair and delivered a scathing, and very loud, speech about how she knew from a friend's experience of health care in London how much better Filipino nurses were than UK nurses, particularly at giving 'TLC'. I interpreted for Colin and Ali: Tender Loving Care. I remained seated, and with a smile and in a calm professional manner thanked her. I shared how wonderful and kind I had found the many Filipino nurses I had worked with in the UK. She attempted to rise again, but the Manila University Dean gently indicated she should remain seated and quiet. She remained a maleficent presence throughout the meeting, but in a way her inappropriate outburst seemed to make the others present more eager to be helpful.

After three days, we had discovered that there was no available proof that Chua had trained in the Philippines, as the College stated on his certificate no longer existed.

However, we felt reassured about the current Philippines nurse training situation. In 2002, with new regulation, a national examination had been introduced to bring educational requirements in line with EU requirements, and nurse registration records were centrally kept. Colleges with an unacceptable failure rate at final examinations had been closed.

We were ready to return home. Colin offered to send the Embassy car to take us from the hotel to the airport. I foolishly declined. We arrived at the airport to find the entrance blocked by thousands of people, all pushing to get past a police check point! Many Filipinos are quite short in stature and Ali and I towered over them. We were spotted by an eager policeman who came rushing over, hand out, saying did we want him to get us through. I very calmly handed him a Peso note, and we soon found ourselves in the relative calm of the international terminal. Ali, with her British sensitivities, was scandalised, asking how I could have bribed an official. I firmly stated it was a tip, and followed this up with the direct question,

"Did you want to miss the flight?"

"No!" was her definitive answer.

The second largest group of diaspora nurses working in the UK are from India. This was therefore our next required destination. I had visited India many times. My first visit in 1982 was to stay with a friend of my parents, who was living in Kerala. Although he has since sadly died, I was delighted to discover that this beautiful state was to be mine and Ali's second destination, as Kerala is the source of the majority of Indian nurses working in the UK. We had also discovered whilst meeting nurse leaders in New Delhi, that out of all the 29 Indian states, Kerala was thought to have the most controlled systems for the education and regulation of nurses.

Ali was not a big fan of India, finding the humid heat exhausting and hating spicy food! She lived on bread rolls. It was with excitement that, on our Sunday off, I dragged a hot and hungry Ali to visit memory lane with me. We walked Kovalam lighthouse beach, no longer the quiet expanse of sand I remembered, but bustling with beach-side shops. I was disappointed, but Ali was delighted by the English menu at the local five-star hotel! This was certainly a very different experience from my 1982 low-budget visit.

We were escorted everywhere by the British High Commission health team, and all doors were open to us. We returned reassured that Indian Nurses from Kerala, and some other states, had certainly received the education required to safely register and thus practice in the UK.

Ali and I saw some very good regulatory practice on our travels, but what did concern us, in a number of countries, was that there were no systems in place for removing a nurse from that country's register if they were unfit or unsafe, even if guilty of murder!

This made it even more vital for us, at the NMC, to strengthen our UK processes for accepting overseas registered nurses onto the UK NMC register. There was no doubt that these fact-finding international visits had been worth the effort.

Shortly after these visits I decided time had come for me to resign from the Council, as new exciting opportunities were calling me. I still believe that when I left, the NMC was in a far better place than when I had joined the original Council. I always hope I played a small part in those improvements, but as with many public service positions it was a team effort. The greatest praise has to go to the CEO and staff team who, for the sake of the British public and for the pride of nursing, worked tirelessly to turn things around.

As well as considering my role within the NMC as a regulator, it is also important to consider what regulation meant to me as a registrant. I have been a proud registered nurse since 1981 and must admit that throughout my working life I rarely questioned my own competence and capability to safely practice, until that is the year of the Covid-19 pandemic.

In 2020, two years after retirement, life became surreal. In January I celebrated my 60th birthday in Edinburgh with 12 friends. In the February, I received my OBE from Princess Anne and 50 friends joined me and the family for a lunch at the Barbers Hall. Then, in March, Covid-19 hit and the world changed.

I had just returned from a working trip to Somaliland and Ethiopia, and within a week had full blown Covid-19, probably caught from an Italian doctor in Addis Ababa. Diagnosis was symptomatic with a very high temperature and a persistent cough, and at the time the unidentified symptom of loss of smell. I complained to my sister that the 'cheer you up' hyacinths she had left for me had no fragrance, and I poured a whole bottle of albas' oil on my pillowcase rather than a few drops, thinking it had weakened in strength over time – my bedroom still stinks of it.

On day seven I thought I was better, and then in week two the high temperature returned with a productive cough, breathlessness, and chest pain. I had developed pneumonia. My respiratory nursing experience came in very useful, and I believe saved me from hospital admission. I continued to strictly isolate, seeing no-one, started Forced Expiratory Technique physiotherapy and rapidly obtained antibiotics, monitoring my own oxygen saturations! General recovery took about four weeks although the breathlessness did persist and was evident for about four months, especially when Zoom recording hymns for the church choir!

As I was recovering, the call came for retired nurses to return to practice. A quandary which led to many hours of reflection. I was still on the nursing register and had always continued practice in a small way, most recently in low-income countries, but I had not hands-on nursed adults since 1982! I decided to 'have a go' at online learning packages related to general nursing, to self-assess my knowledge base. Having achieved over 90% scores in the first six packages I accessed, the indecision increased. My heart told me that I must volunteer, as how could I just sit at home when the NHS was seeking help? There was also the reassurance, at the time but later questionable, that I had had Covid-19, so I'd be at lower risk.

I started to rationalise what help I could be. I knew I could still deliver compassionate, basic nursing care. I was a fast learner and indeed I had the self-confidence to refuse to do anything I was unsure about, or so I thought! I signed up and, having cleared all the red tape, I found myself in the car going to my first night shift on a District General Hospital Covid-19 ward.

It was a traumatic night in many ways. I felt competent and confident interacting with very sick and anxious patients, and delivering end-of-life care, but there was a feeling of panic and utter chaos within the ward. I could hear the staff nurse muttering about my slowness. She was right.

I couldn't find anything. Notes and charts were in four different places and drug administration was a major nightmare and took me forever. The drug charts were 10-page badly written booklets, and the copious drugs required were to be found in five different illogical locations. Indeed, after extensive and prolonged looking, one drug had apparently not been ordered and had to be sourced from ICU. True to my training and risk-averse approach, I was determined to not give drugs I did not recognise or know about, but there was no hard copy formulary as all information was only online, and as a temporary staff member I had no IT access.

I repeatedly tried to seek assistance and explain my limitations, but to no avail. The permanent staff did not seem frantically busy, just unhelpful and dismissive. The only summary can be that I survived the 13-hour shift, and believe I gave not only safe but also compassionate care.

I had no break but spent any spare time sitting with, and reassuring terrified patients, making them copious cups of tea. One patient in the early hours movingly shared with me his horror of watching mortuary trollies coming and going, taking away patients who had succumbed to the same virus he was fighting.

The final straw for me was at morning handover. I was told by the night staff nurse to just handover care that I had given overnight, as the day staff had been on the evening before and knew the patients. She then left early with no words of thanks, and I found myself, alone, handing over the care of my six patients. I was totally taken aback when, rather than expressing any gratitude for work done, the day nurse in charge verbally attacked me, publicly berating me because I had not read the patient's medical notes overnight and could not tell her the full long-term medical history of each patient. I was aware she was playing to her audience of 12 junior nurses and decided I neither had the strength nor desire to retaliate. I just wanted to go home and cry!

The situation was softened when a health care assistant, who had observed my night-time efforts and the handover interaction, sought me out in the changing rooms to tell me to ignore the day nurse in charge as she was a bitch to everyone. I appreciated his reassurance, but still wept on my way home. That night shift could have been my last foray into 2020 nursing, but I am resilient and stubborn.

After food and sleep it was time for reflection and personal honesty! Ward nursing was no longer how I remembered it. Yes, patients still needed caring and compassionate nurses, but I had been totally naïve to believe I could walk onto an acute ward in a 2020 general hospital and slot in. If I was to be of use as a registered nurse in the Covid-19 crisis, or indeed if I was to psychologically survive, I needed to rethink my approach. I needed a positive environment where I was supported, but could also support others, and a role that better suited my personality and skill set. A role where I could safely practice as a registered nurse. This was not a time in life to face a fitness to practice panel at the NMC!

Such a role was awaiting me. The week after the disastrous night shift I was invited to join the team at the Nightingale Hospital in Manchester. This 750-bed field hospital had been built in the Manchester Convention Centre, to care for patients from hospitals across the NW who required intensive rehabilitation after Covid-19. I had the honour of being asked to establish and lead a Family Liaison Team to help isolated patients keep in touch with their families. Many families had last seen, or even spoken to their sick relatives as they were driven away in an ambulance, unsure if they would survive. This role was a perfect fit.

As a paediatric nurse, family-centred care was an ethos I totally understood, and after 40 years in the health service I had vast experience of communicating with the anxious and distressed. As a retiree, with no interest in personal advancement, my only motivation was the welfare of individual patients and their families, even if this meant safely bending the rules. This gave a freedom that I am sure some colleagues envied.

A rule that one evening I had no hesitation in bending was the policy that relatives could only visit a patient in the Nightingale Hospital if their loved one had been formally declared to be at the 'end of life'. On this particular occasion, the doctors agreed that a lady was dying, but, due to her young age, were hesitating to withdraw all active treatment until they had a second specialist opinion. One evening she was struggling to breath and the on-call consultant and I decided that, even though there was no formal end of life declaration, time had come to support her family in coming in to say farewell. She peacefully passed away that night. The next morning, I and the Consultant were summoned by the management team to explain our breach of policy. I was annoyed and simply stated, "How end of life did she need to be? She's dead."

I have to admit that it was not only personally liberating to know that if 'sacked' I could happily return to retirement, but to also know that whatever my actions at the Nightingale Hospital there was no meaningful sanction that would have a professional impact on me. I was happy, at 61, not to be registered. The only thing that would have personally affected me would have been if I, or the team I was leading, could not have been effective advocates for the patients and their families.

It seems somehow wrong to say 'I enjoyed my time at the Nightingale Hospital', but leading the Family Liaison Team was inspirational. My team were all newly qualified dentists or dental therapists, who because of Covid-19 were unable to practice. These enthusiastic and delightful young people approached the role with a compassion that was humbling. Listening to them on the phone, reassuring anxious relatives when the patients first arrived and observing the daily exchanges with patients and relatives was heart-warming. In any spare moments they took the opportunity to entertain or just be with the scared, lonely, or dying. Nothing was too much trouble.

Secure in the knowledge that I would back them up, they became the voice of the patients and families on ward rounds, and as discharge plans were being agreed. They very quickly earned the respect of all the other health professionals, who had at first shunned the role as superfluous to need.

It was gratifying and, although I hesitate to say in such a situation, it was also fun to be there to support their professional development. They acquired superb communication skills in the most difficult of situations, for example opening their eyes as to how to gain the co-operation and trust of patients with dementia. One very serious young man returned to the desk one day to tell us that he had been unable to complete a video call for one old lady because she had said, "John, I can't call now as someone has pooped in my pants and put them back on me."

We asked what he had said, and were amused by his speedy response, "I hate it when that happens!"

Such patient interactions were my greatest delight. Many had been living in a Covid-19 bubble for weeks, with no knowledge of the outside world. I remember one elderly lady's astonished statement when reading about the worldwide pandemic numbers, in her first newspaper for four weeks, "Do you know, Judith, somebody else has had the same bug as me."

The most moving moments were when patients who had been non-verbal and disinterested in life suddenly, due to the efforts of the Nightingale team, reengaged with life, speaking for the first time to their anxious relatives via the iPad calls, joining in our VE day singsong, or sharing with us their life stories.

The Nightingale Hospital was altogether a very special place. Every member of staff had volunteered to work there, everyone was willing to help and guide, and we together developed the service, with all suggestions welcomed and respected. It represented the best of the NHS. I did feel a bit like 'mother' as most of the staff seemed to be under 30. My evenings in the hotel where lots of us were staying were often spent reassuring the young people as they described harrowing shifts.

At the weekends I returned to my village and observed that many were having a far harder time in the pandemic than me. Some were totally isolated as shielding, others had lost their jobs, or their income had plummeted, and families were struggling with 24/7 childcare, including home schooling!

I found it hard when I saw the suffering of others to be treated as a hero, just because I was working in the NHS. I was especially embarrassed by the attention I received following Granada and BBC news appearances, which led to over 67,0000 Facebook hits.

Being described in one Facebook comment as an 'angel without wings' was just too much! We were all doing a job we had been trained for, and we were being paid.

As a former civil servant, I was suspicious of the government support of this hero worship and the messaging related to 'Protect the NHS', which I felt was manipulating and even abusing the public's loyalty to the NHS. It meant people who really needed to access the health service were hesitating. Only a small percentage of the UK's 670,000 registered nurses and 270,000 doctors who were actually working with Covid-19 patients deserved the hero status.

This all-encompassing hero approach for me also overstated the risk of an illness that only had a <2% mortality rate. It encouraged and provided scared health professionals with justification to abdicate their responsibilities, or to deliver suboptimal care by refusing to have face-to-face consultations, allowing mainstream vital NHS services to collapse.

This particularly impacted on my family as, as we had entered lockdown, my brother-in-law was ill, and even though my sister was a retired medical consultant, all her attempts at getting a GP to actually see him had failed. It was only after four months of constant pestering that he was diagnosed with late-stage cancer, and in spite of efforts to then treat him, he very sadly died in the November, during the second lockdown.

I recognise that, due to my global work, I may have an unusual view on professional duty, which includes a registered health professional having to manage risk by protecting themselves as best they can, rather than withdrawing from delivering care. 2% is worrying but not as concerning as working in countries where contagious illnesses like Ebola and Marburg, with mortality rates of around 90%, are constantly present.

I actually feel sorry for the fearful nurses who do not understand why, in their eyes, I put myself at risk working with Covid-19 patients. I can as a Nightingale nurse only respond that I was abiding by my professional Code of Conduct, and it was, therefore, whatever the personal outcome for me, just my job and my duty.

CHAPTER 8

CONVERGENCE OF FLIGHT PATHS

- Chief Executive Officer (CEO) 2014–2018 – (Royal College of Paediatrics and Child Health (RCPCH))

Awards/Honours:

2016 – Freeman of the Worshipful Company of Barbers 2016 – Freeman of the City of London

2018 – RCPCH Children and Young Peoples Voice Award

2018 – Honorary Fellow of the Royal College of Paediatrics and Child Health 2018 – Named as one of 70 Inspirational Nurses who have shaped the NHS

2019 – Officer of the Order of the British Empire (OBE) – for Services to Healthcare

In 2014 an amazing opportunity arose that was to allow me to end my working life in a role that required convergence of all the knowledge and skills I had developed throughout my thirty-six years of work. The Royal College of Paediatrics and Child Health in the UK was seeking a new Chief Executive. This membership organisation is responsible for the training and education of all children's doctors in the country, for improving paediatric care, and for promoting child health in the UK and further afield.

Throughout my career I had always interviewed well, but on this occasion, because I really wanted this post, I felt I floundered. I was therefore absolutely thrilled when three hours later, when sitting at London City Airport awaiting a flight to an NMC Council meeting in Edinburgh, the President rang to offer me the post. I treated myself to a glass of champagne before boarding! I decided to enjoy the next two days inwardly digesting this great news and planning how to inform the unsuspecting London South Bank University Team. I was, therefore, annoyed that by the time I had landed an hour later, news of my appointment had been leaked and was on Twitter. I've never been a fan of Twitter!

After a hurried formal dinner, which had been pre-arranged as my 'leaving do' from the NMC Council, I gave my apologies, boarded the sleeper train at Waverley Station and hurriedly returned to London.

I have to be honest, it gave me great delight to be able to inform the Vice Chancellor, with whom relationships were strained, that I was leaving for a more senior, better paid post.

The RCPCH is a young College, only receiving its Royal Charter in 1996. Its 'Paediatric' rather than 'Paediatrician' title conveys paediatricians' acceptance of the multidisciplinary nature of paediatric care. Although the impact of my nursing background was a question repeatedly asked by the professional press when I was appointed, it never seemed to be an issue for the medical membership. To the contrary, I believe that my being a paediatric nurse was seen as a great advantage. I understood the clinical world in which the members strived to care for children; the opportunities, limitations, challenges, and indeed stresses they faced. When travelling for meetings with members around the UK, I was eagerly taken to see clinical areas, and it was frequently in the middle of a doctors' working environment that I learnt what was really on the doctors' minds. The members accepted me as a paediatric colleague, as well as the CEO of their College.

In the first week I was to discover that the majority of the membership were, however, less eager to accept nurses as members of the RCPCH. The President at the time, Hilary, who is incredibly bright, committed to paediatrics, and a true visionary, had proposed that the RCPCH should be totally restructured to be truly multidisciplinary. On my third day in post, this proposal was rejected in one of the most uncomfortable events I had ever attended.

My role at the extraordinary general meeting was purely as returning officer, announcing the voting results. I was taken aback by the gloating and self-congratulatory behaviour of some of the winning members, even when they witnessed the disappointment and even distress of the President.

It was fortunate that I had previously worked with, and in fact managed Hilary when we both worked at Great Ormond Street Hospital, and I knew her well enough to be supportive. I was obviously, as a nurse, also disappointed that her master plan had been rejected. I agreed with her that the RCPCH should one day play a more strategic part in the education and support of paediatric nurses, but Hilary was ahead of her time. She was cross when I tried to share the 'right time' lessons of patience that I had developed as a civil servant. She stormed from my room, slamming the glass door to my office. This was not the last time as CEO I wondered about the safety of glass doors!

The failed restructure vote left the College membership divided, and members questioning the governance of their College. This in a strange way probably meant frontline members were more interested in what was happening at the College than they had been for many years. Not one to miss an opportunity I decided to grasp the nettle and look at restructuring the College Governance structure. My time at the NMC had taught me so much about good governance of a charity, and the RCPCH needed sorting.

The Council was too large, badly attended, and seemed ineffective. I was determined to hear ideas for a way forward from the frontline members, not just the College's 'great and good'. For the next six months I travelled tirelessly around the UK, flip charts in hand. It was such fun, and my admiration and liking of frontline paediatricians soared!

Attendance varied from 1 to 40 but common sense abounded, and we together arrived at a radical new proposed structure; a truly representative members Council of around 25 and a Governance Board of 12. The bravest decision by members was that the Board would be chaired by a non-medic, the first Medical Royal College to make this move.

The members most exciting decision was, however, that Board membership would include a young person to represent our true beneficiaries. This helped to ensure that the RCPCH would no longer rely on the voice of parents to inform our decision making, but we would truly hear and act upon the voice of children and young people. This would not have been achieved without the expertise and passion of our vivacious staff lead, Emma. I had learnt throughout my career that management success is not achieved by personal effort but by appointing, leading, and working with the right people. Emma was the right person.

Within three months she had convinced every department, even the most reticent finance staff, that the voice of children must be heard. She consulted with groups of children and young people around the UK and engaged them in every aspect of our work. They, for example, informed strategic discussion; contributed to the trainees' curriculum and exams; were involved in senior staff interviews; and a junior school class even led a presentation on healthy living to MPs in the House of Commons.

As a previous adolescent ward sister, these contacts with young people were some of my most enjoyable moments at the College. I was inspired by their honest insight and commitment, and at our annual conference their opening speeches always stole the show. Emma did not really need my involvement. I accepted that my allocated role, when groups of young people were working with her in London, was to annoy tourists by physically blocking tables at Nando's because we couldn't book ahead! One of my proudest moments at my last College conference was when young people presented me with the RCPCH Children and Young People's Voice Award.

As paediatricians, all the three Presidents I worked with fundamentally accepted the inclusion of the young people in our work, although it wasn't the first priority for any of them. Presidents changed every three years and with each change came a different focus of interest. For Hilary it was education. For Neena it was research and challenging political inaction on child health. This theme was further expanded upon by Russell with a manifesto focusing on healthy children and young people as the future of a healthy nation.

The passion of all three was admirable, and I totally understood their desire to deliver what they had promised to the members who had elected them. It was a little like being back in the civil service. My role as CEO was to support the Presidents in delivering their manifesto, but without destabilising the core functions of the College. This did lead to some frustrated clashes on both sides, but mutual respect prevailed.

As to manging and leading the RCPCH staff, my senior management experience was invaluable. They were enthusiastic and dedicated to the work of the College, full of innovative ideas, and eagerly participated in any offered development work. I was determined to use all my people management skills to really make the College a great place for all of us to work, and was ably supported and indeed guided in this by the head of HR, Louise. In my third year we gained Best Company accreditation. All the staff had risen to the challenge, with Directors even accepting with good grace my compilation and circulation of an annual Directors 'Christmas elf dance'!

We had monthly staff get-togethers, annual away days in memorable locations like the zoo and Tower of London, and once a year a party for all the staff's children. As a cake lover I was very happy to judge the staff 'Bake Off' competitions. The Christmas jumper contests were slightly trickier as entries were all impressively outrageous, and the Christmas party brought out the disco diva in the most unlikely staff members.

When I started the staff did sometimes need reminding that I was the boss, not the President, but, once established in the role, I was frequently called upon to rescue staff when they felt 'piggy in the middle', unable to deliver or meet the President's or Officers' many demands. This was usually due to a lack of available resources but was sometimes because requested action was not based on all the facts, or was not in the best interest of the whole membership.

There were some tricky times. The junior doctor pay dispute in 2016 was a particularly 'interesting' episode. The Secretary of State, Jeremy Hunt, tried to impose a new junior doctor contract and this led to a series of strikes, including an unprecedented total withdrawal of labour, by trainees.

The RCPCH President at the time, Neena, was a powerful advocate on behalf of the trainees, passionate about acknowledging their worth and protecting their rights. I thoroughly enjoyed using the knowledge I'd gained when working as a civil servant to explain to her the vagaries of ministerial interactions, and in supporting her as we tried to manage and manipulate contract discussions. We were frequently summoned into the presence of the Secretary of State. Neena rapidly grasped that it was pointless and, in a way, counterproductive to launch into making demands in these meetings.

Demands would be ignored.

The meetings were annoyingly far more about providing the SoS with the ammunition to say, to the worried public, that he had met with the Presidents to gain their assurance that patients would not suffer due to their College's trainees' actions. We could easily and happily provide this assurance for paediatrics, but we were not prepared to be used as a publicity pawn by Ministers.

Neena provided unwavering support for the trainees. After one summons to meet the SoS in his Palace of Westminster office, so well away from prying eyes, Neena marched us straight to the picket line outside the Department of Health on Whitehall so that we could report back on our meeting and be photographed with the demonstrating trainees. The junior doctors can only be described as delighted to see us, but we soon realised that a selfie just wouldn't work, and finding a willing camera operator proved difficult. Neena approached and was rudely shunned by two dark-suited civil servants who were exiting the Department of Health. I was then approached by two young non-English speaking tourists asking for 'Downing Street', and a deal was struck. The picture was taken and by the time we had returned to the College offices we had become Facebook famous!

A further extremely challenging time as CEO of the College was in 2018, when a paediatric trainee was removed from the medical register by the General Medical Council. Dr Bawa-Garba had been in her sixth year of the eight-year paediatric training when, in 2015, she was found guilty of gross negligence manslaughter. This was such a sad situation that I could see from so many perspectives. On a human basis I was devastated for the loving parents of six-year-old Jack Adcock, who had died at Leicester Royal Infirmary in 2011 after a 'catalogue' of mistakes.

I also, however, had sympathy for Dr Bawa-Garba. I am sure that she never meant to harm Jack, and indeed her colleagues described her as an excellent, kind, and caring paediatrician who was distraught about Jack's death. Yes, she had made errors, but I agreed with the Medical Practitioners Tribunal's (MPT) 2017 conclusions that Dr Bawa-Garba's actions were neither 'deliberate nor reckless'. As a previous NHS Trust Director, having read the Trust's internal investigation, I strongly felt Dr Bawa-Garba had been 'scape-goated' by the Trust for systemic failures. Vital IT systems had failed; senior support was unacceptably unavailable; she had worked a 13-hour shift without a break, and had received no induction even though she had just returned from maternity leave to a hospital which was new to her.

As a former Chair of a Professional regulator, I could also appreciate the problem then faced by the doctors' regulator, the General Medical Council, whose primary function is public and patient safety. The public knew Dr Bawa-Garba had been found guilty of gross negligence manslaughter and would therefore struggle with accepting her caring again for their beloved children after only one year's suspension. This suspension time had been the recommendation from the MPT, who in their report had concluded that Dr Bawa-Garba did not 'pose a continuing risk to patients'. It was a mess, and I felt and still feel that Dr Bawa-Garba should never have been charged with a personal criminal offence.

As the CEO of the RCPCH, in 2018 I was involved in many meetings to try and get justice for Dr Bawa-Garba. They varied from sensible discussions to a Sunday morning bullying phone call to my home number, demanding the college supported the GMC position. The phone call was rapidly ended, and an email apology appeared on the Monday. On appeal, in August 2018, the High Court set aside the sanction of erasure.

Dr Bawa-Garba was reinstated by the GMC, which meant that after the year's suspension she could again practice. What continues to sadden me is that Jack's family are unlikely to ever forgive her.

What was interesting during this fight for justice was the antagonistic attitude of the members towards the College. Members, aggrieved on Dr Bawa-Garba's behalf, did not seem to recognise that we were on their side. This was highlighted one day when I received a phone call from an anxious RCPCH receptionists, saying that an angry crowd of doctors, waving placards, were blocking the College entrance. I immediately went down to deescalate the situation, invited the protesters in, offering them coffee, a place to relax and the use of toilet facilities. They seemed amazed, but I was not sure why as many of them were our members and, therefore, this was their building, and I was their staff member! I spent thirty minutes chatting with them about the case, reinforcing our support for Dr Bawa-Garba and they left full of thanks!

Generally convincing the members that the RCPCH was there for them, and that the annual membership fee was worth paying, was an interesting challenge. They seemed to accept that the majority of College activity, and thus income, was committed to the education of paediatricians. Indeed, the education team were so effective and so well led by the Director and her team, that I rarely had to intercede. I enjoyed celebrating their successes, and with my education background felt comfortable in their world, providing a listening ear, and hopefully offering sensible advice if issues did arise. My priority with this team was trying to make sure that they never felt taken for granted.

The most difficult area of RCPCH educational activity was looking wider than paediatricians. In my years in NHS paediatrics, I had observed that once under the care of a paediatrician, children would be appropriately and safely cared for. However, sick children have to reach a paediatrician.

Referrals to paediatricians are mainly in the hands of the GPs. I was, therefore, horrified, when I became the RCPCH CEO, to be informed that Paediatrics was not a requirement in GP training, even though approximately a third of patients that a GP sees, once qualified, are under sixteen years of age. Some GPs would enter practice having only ever had two weeks' paediatric education whilst medical school undergraduates.

Facts like these can cause dismay, but I had learnt over the years to pause before reacting. I soon realised I was not alone in being concerned. The RCPCH education team were working with motivated GP colleagues to address the issue within the GP training curriculum. This, however, did not solve the immediate problem, and

I was excited when Hilary shared with me a project she had initiated with the American Academy of Paediatrics (AAP). They wanted to develop a UK version of the American online paediatric care tool.

The idea was to bring together evidence-based guidance that would allow any UK user to assess a child and arrive at a diagnosis and treatment plan. The UK Paediatric Care Online (PCO) tool journey was to prove tortuous and exasperating.

The Americans were convincingly supportive until money matters entered discussions. Content development and sharing went reasonably smoothly, but over the three years face-to-face meetings had to be held, either side of 'the pond', to decide about ownership, marketing, and shared income. The first time I accompanied Hilary to the Chicago headquarters I soon grasped that we had a fundamental problem. Hilary is a truly dedicated, altruistic UK paediatrician who wants to believe the best of people. The clinical team in the AAP were on the whole a delight, but the lead was an American businessman. He was superficially pleasant and believable, but inherently manipulative, and solely focused on reaching a good economic deal for the AAP.

Negotiating, over the next three years, I certainly needed the support of my very experienced Director of Business Development, Jonathan. In a strange way I thoroughly enjoyed the buzz of entering the fray each time we met our American colleagues. I prepared for meetings as though I was investigating a complex research question. I realised that the extensive people, resource, and risk-management skills I had developed over my career could easily be applied to business management.

Step by step we managed to deliver a bespoke UK decision support tool, but by the time of our final meeting in Vancouver, Hilary was no longer President. Neena, the new President, had no personal commitment to the initiative. At a very confrontational and unpleasant meeting, she made it blatantly clear that she had no desire to be 'friends' with the Americans. At the time I was furious that she had destroyed years of bridge building, but in fact it was her hard-hitting relationship that was needed to move the UK away from American control, and more importantly to stop paying for unnecessary American input.

The UK PCO did however still need funding. The commitment of paediatricians shone through as the members grudgingly accepted a rise in fees to pay for the development and availability of the tool, even though as experts in paediatrics it was not really of value to them. After all this effort, and because I still believe that this was a high-quality and invaluable product that could have transformed frontline access to safe paediatric care, it was with great sadness that after I retired, I was informed that uptake of PCO by other health professionals was so poor that it was being shut down.

I could still cringe as a CEO at the amount of money that I now feel was wasted on the now aborted PCO project, but as an individual I also selfishly reflect back on the opportunities it opened up for me as an individual to travel to America. Chicago in December was certainly an experience. It was deep in snow, and so perishing cold that people were skating on Lake Michigan. Our hotel was in a suburb and just 500 yards from the headquarters of the AAP. On our first morning the hotel offered to book Hilary and me a taxi to take us the 500 yards. We laughed and naively said we needed fresh air

Fresh was an understatement. It was painful it was so cold, so we took the quickest route across a field of snow. We thought the locals were very friendly when two winter-clad individuals were waving from the entrance to the AAP headquarters. When we arrived, we discovered that far from being friendly they were attempting to warn us that our route was not a field but an unstable frozen lake. The next day we took a taxi. As true tourists, however, we did not let the extreme cold, at minus 16 degrees centigrade, stop us taking an open bus tour of the city before our flight home. Most of the subsequent PCO meetings were in Washington DC. I learnt the joys of Segway travel in a stunning and fascinating city where you can walk for miles!

Most of my travel during my time as CEO was around the four UK countries. I knew from my years in the NMC how important it was for true membership representation to not become England-, or indeed London-centric. There were many times when I would have preferred to stay at home base, but I also knew from previous roles that, when building trusting working relationships, nothing replaces face-to-face contact and the opportunity for informal networking. Discussing the amusing misdemeanours of offspring, sharing holiday horror stories, partaking of a G and T or even a fried Mars Bar, all came into the role. I had also learnt in my Civil Service days the value of long journeys for the reading of the 'too hard', or 'too boring' piles of documents.

My previous overseas travel history and international contacts also came to the fore during these three years. We had members from around the world, including a large Indian diaspora, and I was very grateful for the support of my previous High Commission contact, Himanji, when organising a visit for myself and Neena to India. On these visits, cutting through red tape and having meaningful and honest discussions, is certainly more about who you know, not what you know.

Some of the people I met were awe-inspiring, and some of the locations overwhelming. I was at times extremely grateful for the self-belief and self-confidence my parents and indeed my Nightingale training had instilled in me.

Walking into Buckingham Palace for our annual meetings with Princess Anne, our patron, all felt a bit unreal, but was certainly always thought-provoking. I had learnt my lesson at GOSH that she would be well prepared, and I arrived ready to be 'examined'. We were warmly welcomed, she appeared genuinely interested, and asked some very challenging questions.

My admiration for the Princess Royal soared even higher when I received my OBE from her in 2019, and she used the opportunity to briefly discuss the state of child health and the current public health challenges.

A further royal-related honour was in 2017 when I helped to organise, and then attended, a St. George's House event. Set in the grounds of Windsor Castle, St George's House is available for 'groups of a people who are in a position to make a difference …

with issues pertinent to our contemporary world'.

Neena brought together from around the world experts on reducing childhood obesity. We spent three days virtually locked behind the castle walls, considering international evidence, and trying to influence UK policy makers. I am not convinced that the uptake of the outcomes was worthy of the invested effort, but on a personal basis it was an unforgettable experience, topped by a private tour of St George's chapel. I was honoured to be included, and indeed the most unexpected realisation was that I had suddenly become one of the people to be included in such gatherings.

In 2016, I was surprised to be invited, after interview, to be a Freeman of the Worshipful Company of Barbers. This is a London Livery Company established over seven hundred years ago. Membership, originally comprising of barbers and surgeons, now mainly includes medical, financial, and legal professionals. I became the first nurse to join. The Company supports charitable causes mainly related to medical education. To accept this honour, I first had to be made a Freeman of the City of London. This would have historically allowed me to; carry a sword; be hanged with a silk rope if I committed murder or treason; and I could be drunk and disorderly and granted safe passage home from the police. Sadly, these no longer apply although I could still, once a year, take my non-existent sheep over London bridge. On receiving this invaluable Freedom, the clerk kindly pointed out to me the casket presented to Florence Nightingale when she received the same honour in 1908.

I had never forgotten my nursing roots, and it was an incredible honour when in 2018 I was named as one of the 70 Inspirational Nurses who had shaped the first 70 years of the NHS.

In 2018, although I was still really enjoying the CEO post, I decided it was time to retire. I had inherited a beautiful home back up North, next door to my sister and family, I knew that I was financially secure, and I wanted to dedicate more of my time, effort, and expertise to voluntary global health activity. I can also admit I was tired, and my efforts to hide from colleagues my lifelong struggle with severe migraines was taking its toll.

Determined to leave the College in a good place, I carefully planned my departure so that I could spend six months supporting Russell as the new President and to give the College time to make sure a new CEO could be appointed to commence the day I departed.

Any personal feeling of loss was certainly buffered by being unexpectedly made an Honorary Fellow of the College. I was surprised at this event when another recipient, an eminent professor of Neonatology, rushed across the room to give me a hug. He proceeded to tell the assembled crowd that I had been the ward sister on his first paediatric ward, and excitedly shared his memories of my role in his training, and of good times. My career had come full circle.

CHAPTER 9

CHARITABLE ACTIVITY

- Team Leader for MASCOT 1984–1990 (Make a Sick Child's Dream Come True)
- Trustee Help 4 Hurting Children (H4HC) in Uganda 2002–2018 (Chair 2013-2018)
- Trustee Tropical Health and Education Trust (THET) 2014–current (Chair 2015-current)

In 1984, whilst I was a paediatric ward sister, I became involved for the first time in charity activity when I started taking children with life-limiting conditions to Disney with a charity called MASCOT (Make a Sick Child's Dream Come True). For the next six years I spent two to four weeks of my annual leave leading UK-wide teams of eight health professionals and 15 children as we visited the sites of Los Angeles and San Diego. The team always included a doctor, ambulance crew, and a variety of paediatric nurses and physios. The children came from across the UK.

We met the children (aged between seven and 16) at the Heathrow Hilton, and having had a handover from the parents, took over their care for the next two weeks. I remain an expert at giving physio and changing continence pads at 30,000 feet! For the staff team these trips were usually enjoyable, but a total eye opener. It is all very well, strictly telling parents the care they need to give their child 24 hours a day, but different living that life. For example, the staff experienced the reality of giving physiotherapy twice a day to a reluctant teenager, when you are both desperate for a lie-in, or exhausted after a day at Disneyland.

The staff that struggled most were the doctors, and on occasions they negated their responsibilities to others, or tried to opt out. Any staff reluctance, or weakness, was invariably picked up by the children, and the staff member was then the first to be pushed in the pool or taken repeatedly on the most hair-raising rides. One doctor was particularly disliked, and the day of greatest amusement was a visit to Sea World in San Diego. The group were standing around a circular dolphin pool, and one of the dolphins, for no apparent reason, targeted this doctor. Wherever she moved to, this particular dolphin followed, submerged, and rose up with no warning, soaking her each time with spat water!

People question the value of these 'dream' trips, but I saw the transformation in the children we took. For some it was their chance to openly discuss their own deaths, as only children can. One day in the minibus, two terminally ill eight-year-old boys, one from Manchester and another from Liverpool, whose parents had told me at Heathrow that the children were unaware of their poor prognosis, were having a chat about death and whether they wanted to be buried or cremated. The Mancunian boy firmly stated he wanted to be cremated with his ashes scattered on Manchester United's pitch, to which, as quick as a flash, the other replied, "It won't make them play any better!"

We all laughed, but when I turned to the paramedic who was driving, tears were coursing down her face.

In all the years that I led these MASCOT trips, only one child became so unwell that she was admitted to a hospital. Her family were flown out, reassuring me on their arrival that they had known she was extremely poorly. Indeed, to come on the trip they had taken the difficult decision to suspend her place on the UK heart-lung waiting list. It was three days before our return, and she had probably enjoyed the trip more than any other child I had escorted. The day before her collapse, she had been thrilled when we were at Universal Studios, and because she'd had trouble breathing, we had ended up using the oxygen in their First Aid area. Suddenly Angela Lansbury came in. She had been told that there was a very poorly English child in the First Aid room. She was between 'shoots' so had come to keep this child company.

This was one of many acts of kindness we experienced during these trips. One day at Disneyland, a member of their maintenance staff risked disciplinary action when, much to my surprise and the amusement of one of the 15-year olds with Muscular Dystrophy, he replaced a broken screw in his wheelchair and stated,

"Just think, you may be the first young man who says you've had a screw in Disney!"

Disney rules are very strict, and one day I was evicted. One of the 15-year-olds with Cerebral Palsy, Amanda, was desperate to go on the log flume and in a moment of weakness I and a really great doctor,

Lisa, decided we could manage this. All went wrong from the beginning. We got Amanda out of her wheelchair on the moving turn table, me behind her with my arms under her arm pits and holding her wrists to stop her outflying spasms, and Lisa taking her legs. As I stepped down off the moving platform into the log, Amanda fell onto me, and we collapsed onto the long bench seat. Amanda found this hysterically funny, which made her arms go into spasm, trapping my arms under hers.

I was very aware from my numerous trips that the first part of the ride was a rapid ascent before plummeting down into a water-filled pool. Realising that, with my arms pinned, I would not be able to grip the flumes side safety bar, I could visualise us both diving out of the flume as it dropped. We were rapidly approaching the end of platform, and panicking I shouted at Lisa to leap into the front of our log and lie back against us both to weight us down, which she duly did. The log started chugging up the rise, all to the background music of 'zippidy doo da'!

Still unable to release my arms from Amanda's spasmed grip, I decided to hook my leg around the safety bar, and in so doing my shoe flew off into the water, lost forever! As we reached the top and, just in time, I wrenched my arm free and grabbed the bar and we safely descended to Amanda's delighted and excited screeches! The rest of the ride passed without incident, but my concerns were now changed to how we were going to lift her out of the log. I have never been so relieved to see two of our ambulance crew team members on the rotating exit platform, waiting to assist us! Amanda had loved it, and immediately asked to go again, but my nerves just couldn't take it.

I also had a new problem. Disney does not sell any footwear! I ended up having to hobble back to the car park, driving with one shoe to a local mall, buying shoes, and then re-entering!

For Amanda this log flume ride was the highlight of her holiday. It was often the unexpected activity or quiet time that was the most moving to observe. I will never forget sitting in companionable silence with a 14-year-old leukaemia patient, watching the waves crashing onto Venice Beach. Glancing across I realised he was quietly crying. No words were spoken as I hugged him to me. Another evening a member of staff ended up following and gently retrieving a young man who had decided to run away, as he did not want to return to chemotherapy.

The MASCOT trips were all strictly planned but we also tried to respond to specific requests and capitalised on opportunities that unexpectedly arose. One vehicle-obsessed eight-year-old, John, was fascinated by the enormous and very shiny American trucks.

Therefore, one day in a car park, I approached a thickset tattooed truck driver to ask if he could possibly give John, and me, a tour of his truck. He kindly agreed, and even gave us a coke sitting in his spacious cab.

On another trip, one of the children's uncle's was a senior US naval officer. He organised for us all to be given a tour around a naval vessel, with lunch in the Long Beach US naval base canteen. Then before we left, each child was given a US navy belt buckle.

One particularly special memory was linked to my love of

Baywatch, and of course David Hasselhoff! We had decided to have a day with the children on Manhattan Beach, but this came with some difficulty. Wheelchairs are impossible to wheel over sand and one young lady, Lucy, aged 13, who had had bone cancer, had to agree to remove her prosthetic leg as it was an advanced piece of kit, and would not have coped with sand.

Having played an energetic game of rounders, Lucy had won her player of the match title for her ingenious protection of the second base, and I asked what reward she wanted.

"To paddle in the Pacific," was her response.

The sea was a long way out, but I spied a Baywatch-style tower, next to which was parked a rescue vehicle. I wandered over to be met by two lifeguards who would have shamed the Hoff! They immediately agreed to help. I will never forget Lucy's blushes when I arrived in the vehicle and she was swept up by a bronzed Adonis! A dream come true, and the lesson – if you don't ask you don't get!

So many wonderful memories not just for the children, but for all the team members. None of the children we took had ever been to Disney before, and for many it was their first ever holiday. For some it was even the first time they had eaten in a restaurant, or even used a knife and fork. They adapted incredibly fast, and the most moving was seeing how they enthusiastically helped each other.

The MASCOT groups we took always included children from black and ethnic minority groups, and this showed me a side of America I was naively not expecting. In 1992, we were in Los Angeles when riots broke out after four police officers were acquitted of the beating of Rodney King. One of the activities we enjoyed each visit was a trip to a police station in Los Angeles, where the children were allowed to meet police dogs, hold a gun (unloaded!), sit on motorbikes, and use a speed gun on unsuspecting local drivers. This personal contact became invaluable as the Watts riots spread. Each day I received from our police contact updated curfew instructions, and a breakdown of where in LA it was not safe to go. We followed these instructions, but what was incredibly difficult was protecting the two children on our trip who happened to be black. As we arrived at restaurants we were asked to leave as no black people were allowed in. Racist verbal abuse was hurled at the whole group, and on a visit to Griffiths Observatory, when one of our white children went to sit next to a black child on a bench, to innocently play an interactive game together, the panicked mother protectively grabbed her black child, pushing our astonished child to the floor.

I became extremely British, explaining loudly on each occasion that we were British, that these were all our children, and we were certainly not racist. After this trip I began to notice the racist behaviour I had probably been blind to before. One specific incident was entering the Hall of Presidents in Disney, where holograms of past Presidents gave memorable speeches. You may, quite rightly, think not a gripping experience for UK children, but to be honest it provided a very good excuse for a comfortable sit down in the midst of a busy Disney day. The seating was arranged in numerous very long semi-circular rows, with guests expected to fill in from the far end. On this occasion, we entered nearing the start time when many rows were already full, but strangely one row, in a prime position, was almost empty with two ladies at the far end. I eagerly led the way, shepherding our party into this row. When I reached the two seated Americans, and sat down, the nearest lady turned to me.

"I gather that you are English," she said.

I was surprised as I didn't think I was dressed in an obvious UK manner (no knotted handkerchief on my head).

"Yes, how did you know?" I replied.

She just sighed and said, "You sat next to us."

I then realised that they were the only black people I could see in the theatre.

Having lived and worked in large multicultural cities in the UK, I had never, until my time in LA, felt the fear of an outsider due to skin colour. One of the children we had taken on one of our MASCOT trips had had a heart transplant, and unfortunately on day one she dropped the glass bottle containing her essential non-rejection medicine! Having contacted the UK transplant centre, they arranged for us to collect a replacement bottle from the nearest public hospital. Lesley, a UK ambulance officer, and I, dropped all the children and staff back at the hotel after a day at Knottsberry Farm, and wearing our very touristy shorts and Snoopy t-shirts, set off to find the hospital. It was dusk. We parked the minibus in the hospital car park and casually strolled into the main entrance. As we entered the noisy Emergency Room waiting area, silence fell, and around 50 black faces turned to follow us as we walked from the entrance to the bulletproof glass protected reception desk. The receptionist had not seen us as we walked over, but she looked up as I said in a very British way, "Excuse me."

She jumped from her seat, ran to the locked door to the right of the desk, and bundled us inside the locked reception area, pressing a security call button. The medicine was rapidly located, and unnerved, we were escorted by armed security through a service entrance back to our vehicle.

The children were totally mesmerised by the blatant carrying of firearms in Los Angeles, but I don't think I really understood the dangerous environment in which we found ourselves until on one trip, news of a fatal shooting was announced on the minibus radio, only five minutes after we had left the exact location of the incident outside the Chinese Theatre on Hollywood Boulevard.

I realised that, having been caught out by an earthquake whilst we were in LA in October 1987, we always rehearsed with the children the protective action they should take if the ground shook, but we had never planned for a shooting incident! Of course, because so rare in the UK, most of the children found both earthquakes and shooting incidents so exciting that, when parents met them at Heathrow, these events were excitedly described before Mickey Mouse.

Now reflecting back, I am amazed how calmly I accepted all the responsibilities of leading these MASCOT trips. At the time they were the highlight of my year. It was an honour to be part of this life-changing and awesome experience for the children. On a personal note, it taught me so much about how to rapidly pull together, lead, and manage an effective multidisciplinary team, always remembering that we were all volunteers, and it was our holiday as well. I continued leading MASCOT trips until 1990 when I left Booth Hall to train as a Nurse Tutor.

The next time I was tempted back into volunteering my time and expertise to support a charity was in 2001, when I was the Director of Nursing at Great Ormond Street Hospital. From the 1950s until the atrocities of the Idi Amin regime started in 1971, Great Ormond Street Hospital had supported the development and running of the paediatric unit at Mulago Hospital in Kampala, sending two GOSH nurses and two doctors to work in the Ugandan unit, on a two-year rotational basis. These GOSH staff had been withdrawn the day the 'troubles' began, and for the next twenty years Mulago had been struggling to deliver paediatric care.

The initial approach to me for help was from the inspiring Ruth Simms, a senior UK nurse, working in a UK-managed HIV facility in Kampala. Whilst setting up paediatric care for children with HIV, Ruth had realised the lack of paediatric knowledge and expertise in Uganda. Ruth is not someone you refuse. I held out for about a year before capitulating under pressure and setting off for Uganda.

It was my first time in Africa (not counting a week sunbathing in Morocco in the 1980s)! This was to be a life-changing visit. We were shown cramped paediatric wards. Two or three babies in each cot were lying on thin rags placed on the metal bases. Oxygen cylinders were rare, often empty or if available the staff were attempting to share supplies between the gasping babies and children through a multiple taped connector arrangement.

On my first visit to a dingy acute assessment area, I noticed a small unaccompanied child, gasping and wheezing in a wooden wheelbarrow parked in a corner of the room.

There was no oxygen available that day, no drugs to help his breathing and this child, who would in England probably have made a total recovery, was not going to survive. I gently picked him up and rocked him. The staff asked what I was doing. It was with great sadness I admitted I could not save him, but I could at least hold him as he died. I still frequently relive this experience when explaining to people why from that moment I was committed to improving global healthcare.

In 2002, under Ruth's chairmanship, and with the support of four others she had convinced to come on board, the Help 4 Hurting Children (H4HC) charity was founded. The charity, which I was to go on to Chair from 2013 to 2018, aimed to deliver training to Ugandan child health professionals. This also necessitated providing health staff with the basic tools of their trade. I never ceased to be embarrassed when doctors fell to their knees to thank us for a stethoscope, or when I observed the nurses' joy at being given a five-pound fob watch.

As a Director of GOSH there was also the opportunity, when opening newly equipped units, to send across pristine but obsolete larger pieces of equipment. On one memorable Saturday in 2006 we even closed Great Ormond Street and carefully packed an 80-foot container, constantly bearing in mind that we did not want to add to Mulago hospitals equipment graveyard. Mulago, like many hospitals in low-income countries, was sadly full of useless or broken items. Disposable components or a consistent electricity supply were often not available, or an incompatible Ugandan voltage or power supply surge had destroyed any power dependent equipment's working parts.

A sombre illustration of this problem could be observed on the neonatal ward. Staff , thrilled to be given incubators, were still using them even when they were no longer working, and now due to a lack of maintenance the incubators were probably more hazardous for the babies than care in a cot. We gave careful consideration as to what should be sent from the UK and what would, due to cost and availability of parts, be better purchased in Uganda.

Containers were expensive to send, and for the security of the GOSH 2006 donation, I flew out with the padlock keys for a grand opening. I only had a weekend free, so timing was tight, and then overnight we had the worst thunderstorm I had ever witnessed. We worried all night that our plans would be scuppered, but then in the morning the sun shone, and the rain had made our task easier by settling the ubiquitous Ugandan red dust.

The container opening was quite an event, with Ugandan dignitaries not only attending but rolling up their sleeves to help unload and distribute the contents around Mulago. One lesson we did learn was not to send anything heat sensitive as, during transit, particularly in the tremendous heat of Mombasa dock, contents melt. A shipment of nurses' uniforms had to be discarded having arrived fused to their plastic packaging. There was also the ethics of equipment donation to consider. We never sent anything that had been considered hazardous for use in the UK, for example, because out of date.

This may suggest little was sent but these initial and subsequent containers were tightly packed with, for example, nonelectric beds, cots, mattresses, play equipment, etc. The added bonus was that on arrival the containers were themselves used as additional ward or office space. It is still a strange and, in a way, proud feeling to see GOSH labels when I visit Mulago wards.

Ruth's initial appeal for help had, however, not been for equipment. It had been for educational input. It doesn't matter how much equipment you have if staff are unable to assess, recognise, and care for a critically ill child. This was a more difficult request as I realised that, as the Director of Nursing at GOSH, I had little hope of reinstating the permanent placement of paid GOSH staff in Uganda. I equally knew I could not walk away.

Ruth was only asking for help with the periodic paediatric teaching of Ugandan nurses and doctors. This I could help with, not just personally, but by using my contacts to source willing senior paediatric nurses and nurse lecturers from across the UK. Ruth at first provided the teaching facilities in her HIV hospital, and twice a year organised Ugandan attendance at two-week training courses delivered by me and other volunteer UK trainers. When not classroom teaching, these UK volunteers, having registered with the Ugandan regulator, spent any free time working alongside their Ugandan colleagues in Ruth's paediatric wards.

This arrangement in the UK-run HIV hospital was a gentle

introduction. It was so rewarding to see the excellent care the children were receiving, but we realised that our efforts were having a limited, or perhaps no impact on wider paediatric care. The course attendees from Mulago and other Ugandan hospitals seemed to enjoy the training days but, when we visited them in their clinical areas, it was difficult to see any change in practice, due to poor facilities, lack of resources, and low staff to patient ratios. In one hospital I visited there was only one nurse for up to 100 critically ill patients, a sombre comparison to the 1:6 ratio in Ruth's paediatric wards or the >1:4 in the UK.

It was vital for our lesson planning to understand the real-world practice environment for the staff we were now teaching. It was pointless teaching the early warning value of regular observations on every child. The Ugandan staff neither had the time, capacity, nor equipment to deliver this. We learnt the need for two-way listening and learning. We could explain the theory of what to look for to identify if a child was deteriorating, and the Ugandan staff explained how they spotted deteriorating children as they rushed around the ward area.

We learnt not to teach UK procedures that required equipment that was not available, but to work with the nurses to consider what would be possible. For example, in the UK no feed is put down a nasogastric tube without checking a tube is in the stomach by acidity testing aspirated fluid. In Uganda, litmus paper to check the acidity is rarely available.

Together we sought solutions to such safety challenges and the

UK trainers developed their own innovative and flexible thinking. We all returned to the UK with new skills, appreciating and grateful for the UK NHS, and determined to better use the resources available to us.

People in the UK seem to believe that when UK health staff work in low- and middle- income countries it is totally altruistic and of no value to the UK. I can only say that for me my Ugandan experiences changed my whole outlook on healthcare. Yes, some of it was about increased gratitude for the NHS but it also reinforced my passionate support for UK practice that I had until then taken for granted.

One such learning event was a visit to a small storage room in Jinja Children's hospital, where I found six cots tented by draped blankets. When I asked what was within, I was informed that this was the Tetanus ward. Each cot contained two or three small children, and the blankets were in place to reduce any stimulation that could potentially lead to such violent spasms that bones would break. Rarely were any painkillers available and an agonising death was, therefore, the probable outcome. I would never again question the need for tetanus vaccinations.

Indeed, my experience in low-income countries, observing children dying from preventable illnesses like tetanus, measles, and cholera, has made me not just a passionate advocate for vaccination programmes, but angry with those in the UK who refuse what is freely available to protect their own and their children's health.

Uganda was reaffirming my passion for the universal health values of the UK NHS, but was also opening my eyes to global health challenges, not just in large cities but within remote communities.

Working with Ruth's HIV team provided me with the opportunity to accompany the HIV hospitals' outreach team to many parts of Uganda, to help run paediatric outreach clinics. Some areas in the north were at the time too dangerous for us to visit due to the activity of the Lord's Resistance Army (LRA). I really came to appreciate how dangerous when one of the outreach teams returned with a critically ill seven-year-old LRA child soldier, Paul. The Ugandan army had found him unconscious under a tree. Paul had been abandoned by LRA soldiers when he had fallen from a tree whilst being sent to get honey from a hanging beehive. Hitting his head, he had started fitting, a terrifying sight of demonic possession for superstitious LRA soldiers. They ran away.

Paul's story was heart-breaking. Stolen from his family with his little six-year-old cousin, he had been forced by the LRA to maim his own mother by cutting off her breasts, and then, when his cousin had tried to escape, he had been made to join other children in hitting and biting his cousin until dead.

Having woken in safe surroundings Paul refused to speak or eat and was starving himself to death. After many hours by his bed, concerned staff, led by Ruth and Paul's uncle, realised that he had decided he would rather die in this nice place than ever risk being re caught by the LRA. He was eventually convinced by the team that he would be safe and started eating. I hope he has gone on to live a happier life.

Paul's case has remained with me, but the only time that I had flashbacks and debated seeking professional help was after a visit to one of the most beautiful places on earth, but also one of the saddest. The Ssese Islands, an archipelago of eighty-four islands in the north-western part of Lake Victoria, are, in spite of recent palm oil plantation infiltration, still magnificent. Long beaches, beautiful forests, and more exotic birds and monkeys than I have ever seen.

As we left the ferry, we could see the hotel we were to stay in. From a distance it looked idyllic. It was only as we arrived that we realised time had not been kind. The chalets were falling apart, electricity was only available two hours a day, and the only chance of a hot shower was if you paid a little lad to peddle a bike sited next to a water tank which was perched over an open fire. The mosquito nets were in shreds and the beds were black with lake flies.

My two UK colleagues, visiting Uganda for the first time, looked horrified. I set to, shaking off the flies, covering the beds with our own towels and attaching and firmly tucking in our own mosquito nets. Dinner that night was around the beach campfire with large dogs patrolling. One UK colleague, convinced that rabies was a definite risk, was disgruntled at the dogs' presence until she realised that they were vital as a hippo deterrent.

The next day we set up the paediatric clinic overlooking a beach, expecting around 50 children. Small boats, packed with children, appeared from every direction and that day the team saw around 400 children. HIV/AIDS was rife and most of the children's parents were very sick or dead. Child-led families seemed to be the norm, with older children responsible for the care of the orphaned younger ones.

The children rarely had shoes and were clothed in sack cloth, or even adapted mosquito netting, but children will be children. That day as we helped the team assess and treat the children, I longed for a support bra as we joined in many jumping dances and sang until we were hoarse. Frances, the play consultant from Manchester, was with me on the trip. I'll never forget coming out of a circular thatched house she had refused to enter because of rats in the roof, to find her performing 'head shoulders knees and toes', with 30 of the village children.

Happy memories but then came a shock meeting. Unexpectedly we came across a Belgian doctor who had set up a centre to treat abused babies and toddlers who had been irreparably damaged by fisherman who believed that they would be cured of HIV/AIDS if they raped an innocent child. How we longed to put a stop to this abuse, but the harsh reality was that the fisherman paid the head of the child-led family in food. Stop the rape and all the children starved, a conundrum that was beyond anything I had ever come across. I felt powerless and useless and still today shudder at the inhumanity we saw that day.

This could have made us abandon our training trips but what convinced us to continue was the enthusiasm and commitment of our Ugandan colleagues, and indeed now friends. Having gained confidence and contacts, by the time Ruth retired from the HIV hospital in 2010, we had expanded our activity to teach in the National Hospital site at Mulago and at Jinja Children's Hospital.

For many of the nurses and doctors being taught in groups of around 60, this was the first time that they had been taught together.

At first, they were reticent about engaging with each other, or indeed with the lively UK team. We persevered, assisted by senior Ugandan paediatricians and nurse managers, who enthusiastically joined sessions and modelled participation.

Time keeping was probably the most frustrating challenge for the UK team who were used to a prompt morning start. There were no denying excuses for wandering in up to two hours late, were genuine. Some had worked a night shift to gain the time to come; timing travel was a nightmare in a traffic gridlocked Kampala; families had to be sorted. We learnt providing breakfast was a winning tactic, as well as each day rewarding attendees with small pieces of equipment related to the sessions that they had actually attended, e.g., fob watches, thermometers, toys. This was a great plan until it became unaffordable when we started teaching groups of up to 400 in nurse training schools!

Attendees at our sessions were always eager but often exhausted. To earn sufficient salary many worked seven days a week and often double shifts. All seemed to speak English but had to concentrate to understand our British accents. We learnt to pause every twenty minutes for a lively action song, always led by eager and incredibly talented attendees. I learnt many new moves, but my Ugandan never improved!

Help 4 Hurting Children volunteers over the 16 years taught over 4,000 Ugandan paediatric staff, and our fundraisers donated copious amounts of vital equipment. Costs were kept to a minimum. Trustees worked for free, and many volunteers used their annual leave and mainly self-funded their trips. We stayed in basic, but always safe accommodation, organised by our superb administrator, Jessica who to this day remains a good friend. Happy, our driver and guardian, also stays in touch and drives me when I visit Uganda. He is adept at getting me safely from A to B, avoiding dangerous roads and riots, particularly at election times, and we have learnt to carry lemon juice with us in case of tear gas.

The H4HC team in the 16 years never cancelled our biannual visits, even in times of Ebola or Marburg outbreaks, which are a regular occurrence in Uganda. It was this consistency that I think reassured and convinced the staff we really cared. We did care, but we were also extremely frustrated. Each year we dedicated our free time and personal funds to share our knowledge and expertise, but frontline paediatric practice in the main Ugandan hospitals did not generally seem to change.

Ruth, who had now retired from the HIV hospital, came up with an impressive plan.

One of the worst wards in the whole of Mulago was the paediatric malnutrition unit, Mwanamugimu. It had become a forgotten place of sadness, with some babies even dying in their mother's arms as they made the long walk from Mulago's accident and emergency department, up the steep hill to the ward. To the left of the ward entrance was a small room with old wooden shelving, and on these shelves, babies deemed too sick to save were stacked and left to die. Even if admitted to the ward areas, the fight to survive was for many hopeless, and the unit had a 52% death rate. There was frequently no electricity or water, it was filthy, and obviously at the end of the hospital priority list for receiving any oxygen or drugs. However, each day loyal staff struggled to care.

Ruth decided to help. With money and volunteers from her local UK church, and having gained permission and support from President Museveni, the three-year Restore project transformation began. The buildings were repaired and decorated, plumbing replaced, generators installed. The unit was unrecognisable. Essential drugs, oxygen, and lifesaving equipment were made available, and even an ambulance was purchased. This ambulance ensured very sick babies arrived from A and E alive. It was also compassionately used to take the dead home for burial, rather than expecting mothers to carry the little bodies home in a carrier bag on the local matatu (shared minibus taxi).

As well as sorting the material infrastructure, Ruth and her friend Sue based themselves on the unit. They recruited Restore funded volunteer nurses, nutritionists, and play staff, and with funding from a UK donor, Roz, even provided food for all staff and resident carers. The Ugandan team's motivation soared, and Ruth reached out to the H4HC team to deliver biannual training, but this time she provided a constant supportive presence with constant monitoring of practice change. Over the next three years the mortality rate on the malnutrition unit dropped from 52% to 10.7%. All were delighted, and there was even an official reopening in June 2011 attended by the President and attracting wide press coverage.

Then came the difficult day in 2013, when Restore funds had run out. Ruth and Sue, both now unwell, had had to come home to the UK, and although the H4HC team would still visit to deliver training for a further five years, the leadership of the unit was returned to the Ugandan team. Mulago's managers had promised at the outset that once established they would maintain the Restore model of provision, but it soon became apparent that this was not to be. Funding for the Restore volunteers was not forthcoming, and the hand-over party was horrific.

Ruth, who was idolised by the staff, gave an upbeat thank you speech, and then to my horror said to the assembled throng that I would explain what was to happen next. I had expected to just reassure them that the H4HC training would continue, instead of which I found myself forced to tell the staff that there was no longer any money for the 24 Restore volunteers. The response was heart-breaking. I expected anger, instead of which there was calm acceptance, and with the Restore pastors support, we all prayed together that as 'this door shut a new window would open'. For most no window opened, and they voluntarily continued to work every day on the unit for no pay, some for many years.

H4HC was not financially able to rescue the whole Restore team, but we did what we could. Until 2018 Roz continued to pay for the parent and staff lunches, and funds mainly raised from my London church paid for the replacement of essential equipment and vital oxygen and drugs. Jessica, Happy, the pastor, and two other family support staff continued to receive a small monthly allowance.

Each H4HC training visit to Uganda I also, at the insistence of the

Ugandan team, visited the hospital senior Management and pleaded for the remaining Restore staffs allowances to be reinstated, but with no success. I was actually over the time increasingly embarrassed about making these appeals. Yes, the mortality rate on Mwanamigimu had crept up to around 15%, but certainly not the original 52%, and the challenges being faced by the Mulago senior management team were enormous. The visits became more mutually supportive, and for me educative, as I discussed with the Mulago executive team models of funding, how to deliver a wide range of health services, and the practicalities of workforce planning in low-income countries.

It was during these discussions I learnt the term 'ghost-workers'. This referred to people on the payroll who never actually worked in the hospital, apparently a common phenomenon in developing countries, and which the Mulago CEO informed me accounted for around a third of his paid staff. The CEO's approach to address the issue I found startling, but certainly decisive, and in a way brave. Pay for all staff was stopped for around three months, but amazingly the dedicated staff continued to come to work each day. Then, on an unexpected day, barricades were set up at every entrance to the hospital with a register taken of every staff member that turned up for work. None attending staff were permanently removed from the payroll, and the pay for the staff who had reported for their shift was recommenced, although I was never sure the three months back pay was received.

I increasingly became fascinated by the health system challenges faced by the Ugandan management team. I realised that although it had been easy and immediately rewarding to travel out and teach clinical paediatrics, my true expertise was no longer in frontline paediatric care. I could leave this to my young, enthusiastic, and far more up-to- date colleagues.

From 2015, as requested by Ugandan partners, I and a trusted colleague facilitated interactive leadership and change management sessions for senior paediatric managers. On day one I was more nervous than I had ever been delivering clinical sessions. Determined to ensure total applicability to the Ugandan health system, I knew the success of the designed training was totally dependent upon active participation. It was only as the 25 eager attendees entered the room that I realised that my concerns were to be unfounded. I was engulfed in hugs and deafened by excited chatter, soon realising that the vast majority of management attendees at these sessions had previously attended H4HC paediatric training. This was further brought home to me when introduced to a Ugandan Minister at an International conference in London in 2016. She threw her arms around me and thanked me for the training she had received in 2004, when a practising paediatrician.

In 2018, when I retired, we officially finished H4HC training visits, and closed the charity. This was very difficult, but I still believe a correct decision. We knew from the interactions with the attendees on our short courses that paediatric knowledge gained during Ugandan-led training was now quite good. The remaining challenge was putting knowledge into practice, and our biannual visit model of delivery was not going to address this.

In 2013, we had tried to develop a new approach, writing, with Ugandan colleagues' input, a comprehensive paediatric distance learning package that included reflection and a change management approach. I am still proud of what the H4HC team and African colleagues produced, but it is my greatest frustration, and in a way an embarrassment, that I have, in spite of numerous attempts and because of others' broken promises, failed to get the package introduced in any developing country. It sits on my study shelf as a constant reminder of what could have been if I had had true buy in from global partners. We must all learn from our mistakes, and this experience reinforced for me that effective global activity requires respectful partnership, with shared ownership and agreed desired benefits for all parties.

This newfound clarity meant that, in 2014, I was delighted to be invited to become a trustee of the Tropical Health and Education Trust (THET), an organisation that expounds such partnership values. I was even more surprised and honoured when, a year later, I was appointed as the THET Chair. In spite of all my experience and apparent success, and indeed the self-confidence others see in me, I was a bit perplexed to find myself leading and interacting with some of the most senior health professionals in the UK, and indeed the world.

THET was founded in 1988 by the amazing Professor Sir Eldryd Parry. It has over the last 32 years become the 'go to' organisation to manage partnership between the UK and Low- and Middle-Income Country (LMIC) organisations. THET partnerships are primarily aimed at increasing and developing the global health workforce. I am realistic about my role as Chair. It is certainly not about personal glory. I am, unless asked, very happy to stay in the shadows with Eldryd, or our Patron, Lord Nigel Crisp, taking the star roles at public events. I see my role as making sure THET benefits from the contribution of all the excellent Trustees, and that the charity is safely led and governed.

I was realistic from the start that my time commitment as Chair would be taken up with chairing and attending meetings, reviewing policies, acting as a channel of communication between the board and staff, and supporting and supervising the Chief Executive. The latter has been a doddle as Ben, the CEO, is so driven and dedicated to THET's mission. As to policies and chairing meetings, that has been my world for many years so has not presented too many challenges. Neither has interacting with the staff, on the proviso that Ben tells me, and corrects me, if I am straying and interfering in operational rather than strategic activity.

The main challenges have been related to risk management and assurance. This has included addressing concerns about the financial health and sustainability of the charity in the UK, a country where the increasing mantra appears to be 'charity begins at home', and identifying appropriate UK partners and sufficient volunteers when the NHS are continually bleating about staff shortages.

Governance challenges have most often related to the complexity and difficulties of working on a global stage. Natural disasters and internal unrest, for example, riots during elections, military coups or suspected ethnic cleansing are not unheard of in the low-income countries where THET have a presence. Our policies have to be applicable and enforced in many jurisdictions. We have to guard against potential fraud or theft as we manage large grants in countries where money is scarce and therefore temptation sadly understandable, and safeguarding was certainly highlighted as a major consideration when Oxfam hit the headlines in 2017.

Due to the seniority of every Trustee, and the honest endeavour of the THET senior team, each challenge has been handled with calm professionalism and the charity has gone from strength to strength. It is of particular note that in 2020, when many charities were decimated by Covid-19 restrictions, THET was globally accepted as making a positive difference. Problems were shared and solutions found and the 2020 conference, held online, attracted over 450 delegates from more than fifty countries. The global lockdown also brought greater equivalence for every member of the THET team, as, wherever in the world they were based, e.g. a room in London, Yangon, or Hargeisa, they all had the same level of presence and involvement in Zoom calls and meetings.

Being the Chair does not include travel opportunities as a Chair's role is in the UK. However, on three occasions I was able to combine invitations to teach paediatrics with visits to THET in-country teams. This led to a very pleasant return visit to Uganda in 2018, when I was helping the Edinburgh University partners in the delivery of a paediatric palliative care leadership course.

In 2020, it was more daunting when I answered an appeal from a Somaliland nurse leader to travel to her country to deliver paediatric and neonatal training. With support from THET's Somaliland team, and having organised for a paediatric nursing friend, Jenny, to accompany me, I prepared more carefully for this trip than any other in my life. I now realise that my trepidation was due to, not only my own, but everyone else's lack of knowledge and understanding about the independence of Somaliland from the realistically feared Somalia.

Somaliland, a semi-desert territory on the coast of the Gulf of Aden, broke away and declared its independence from the violent, warlord-led state of Somalia in 1991. Despite lacking international recognition, Somaliland now has its own independent government, currency, police, and security system. It has seen little of the violence, extremist attacks, and kidnappings that plague Somalia, but even so before going we were required, for insurance cover, to undertake hostage training. It was certainly unnerving when on arrival we had to accept a six p.m. curfew, carry with us at all times an emergency pack, and learn extraction plans.

In ten days our only foray out of Hargeisa, the capital, was to observe the milking of camels. Interesting, but I am not sure worth the extensive planning for this hour-long trip. Heavily armed security men escorted us as we left the city limits. The scenery was limited, and we weren't actually allowed to try the camel milk as it makes foreigners very sick!

The whole Somaliland trip was a strange psychological mix. I have never felt as warmly welcomed, or indeed as impressed by the total commitment of absolutely everyone we met to strive tirelessly to achieve success for their country. What had been achieved in 27 years was amazing. I remember standing on my hotel balcony in Hargeisa comparing the view of the bustling city before me, with a 1990 photo of totally flattened rubble.

Everyone we met had a story to tell. Stories of fleeing at the height of the conflict, across miles of desert to the relative safety of Ethiopia or Djibouti, and stories of family members lost. The most traumatic shared memory was of finding the mass graves of children who had been buried alive, having been exsanguinated and rendered unconscious by the Somalia army when requiring blood for injured soldiers. A young waiter at the hotel told of how his mother instructed him to appear sick and weak when at school, so that when Somalia troops entered classrooms to source new donors he would not be chosen.

Hearing such stories, not told to shock but as statements of fact, made us even more in awe of the positivity of the people we met. We found ourselves bewildered and in our own way annoyed that the world would not recognise Somaliland as independent from Somalia. We knew this was way beyond our sphere of influence, but so wanted to help this country, a country where poverty in rural areas was still running at 38% and where the Maternal and Child Mortality rates are some of the highest in the world. We could try and share our knowledge of evidence-based paediatric and neonatal care, we could model good practice, even singing nursery rhymes to demonstrate, to a staggered audience, the power of distracting children from painful procedures. What we could not even hope to address were the challenges of which we had no knowledge, for example, the horrific practice of female genital mutilation, inflicted upon 98% of Somali women, or the long-term impact of surviving in a war zone.

As Chair of THET I kept asking all I met what partnerships they felt would be helpful, and the appeal from the head of the Somaliland Nurses Association was something I could help with. Because Somaliland was not a recognised country, they had been refused admission to the International Council of Nurses (ICN). On my return to the UK, I presented Somaliland's case to the ICN CEO, who was luckily a former nursing colleague. The response was immediate, and the plea was heard and accepted. Somaliland is now a member of the ICN, giving them access to international nursing support.

It was very clear on our trip that nurses and indeed the whole Somaliland health service do need international help. In the Hargeisa hotel we met some of the volunteers from Kings College in London, who have been a constant and vital presence since Somaliland independence was declared. It was a member of the Kings team that was my pre departure guide to the purchase and wearing of suitable garments for my trip. This included providing lessons on the wrapping and firm fixture of hijabs.

Somaliland has extremely conservative Islamic requirements for female attire. We were assured that we did not have to wear a Niqab or Burka face covering, but the abaya had to cover all the way to the wrists and ankles, and the hijab had to be tightly wrapped to hide every hair, and then draped to mask any female curves. Donning this garb for the first time in the toilets at Addis Ababa airport, before boarding the Somaliland flight, was a challenge, but help was accepted from two Somali ladies, who found our feeble attempts highly amusing!

By the end of the 10 days, we were highly accomplished at hurriedly donning the required garments, as they even had to be worn if opening a bedroom door. The abaya was extremely comfortable, and strangely cool in the very hot conditions, but I have to say that at the end of a day's teaching in stifling hot rooms, we longed for our private HFT (hijab-free time) and a shower.

Our female students were all similarly attired with some also wearing Burkhas, which I must admit made teaching tricky. When trying to understand participants' questions or responses, it was hard enough understanding the accented English, but almost impossible when sound was muffled, and we could not lip read. Solutions can always be found, and although the 50% male attendees chose to sit at a distance from the women, they, and the Burkha-free women, became willing interpreters.

We felt we were adapting well. Then, one day, when out at a café with one of the male UK doctors, a stranger approached him to say he found it insulting that the non-Muslim Western women were wearing traditional Somaliland dress. This was a conundrum for us. We had dressed this way out of respect, and I suppose for our own safety, certainly not to insult. It was at times like this that the advice and support of THET's in-country team was so invaluable, and we continued to be fully covered until casting aside the hijab on the plane back to Addis.

I have to admit our first night in Ethiopia, dressed in cotton summer dresses, and sipping a Gin and Tonic after an unescorted wander around the city, was a good feeling. Due to Jenny's UK work commitments we sadly only spent three days in Addis Ababa, meeting the THET Ethiopian team, and discussing partnership requests with Ethiopian ministers and officials. One day I will definitely return as a tourist.

Myanmar was somewhere else I had never considered visiting, but somewhere that my friend Kathy had decided she wanted to visit, having heard all about it from a Burmese friend at her church. In 2017, I, Kathy, her sister Liz, and our friend Janice, my regular holiday gang, decided to book a two-week tour. At the time I was the CEO at the Royal College of Paediatrics and Child Health (RCPCH), and the College had been working with the Myanmar Paediatric Society since 1998. In 2017, the MPS were exploring the need to increase paediatric training of nurses.

THET also had an office in Myanmar. I decided I would grasp the opportunity to travel to Myanmar 10 days ahead of my friends to support both the RCPCH efforts and to meet the THET team.

It was an exciting prospect as I had for years heard my Uncle Jack's stories of being in Burma during the war. He had been an army officer, involved in recruiting and training Nigerian troops, and then leading them into battle against the Japanese in Burma, where he sustained an injury leading to the loss of a finger. He was, by 2017, in his 90s and bed bound, but totally 'with it'. In conversation I told him I was going to visit Burma, and he immediately reminisced about the kindness of the people and the beauty of the valley of 2,000 temples, Bagan.

"Give my regards to my finger," he said with a twinkle in his eye.

How right he was about Myanmar. The country is not just beautiful, but totally fascinating. The people we met whilst travelling were a delight. We were invited into people homes to share Myanmar snacks, invited to join wedding parties, and even helped wash elephants in a fast-flowing river.

The locals were fascinated by the sight of four English ladies travelling alone. A particularly memorable experience was sitting on low stools with six Inle Lake lady lotus flower spinners and chatting about our very different lives. We saw numerous Buddha's of every shape and size, and became adept at shoe removal, regretting pre-holiday pedicures that had removed essential hard skin from the soles of our feet!

The faith of the people appeared all consuming, with even the poorest offering gifts to Buddha. For the first time I understood the importance of the short time most Burmese spend as monks or nuns during childhood, developing prayerfulness, and an acceptance of the importance of charity giving and the humility of receiving. What was difficult to accept was the abject poverty we observed in the remote regions.

In rural areas we saw farming practices, and cottage industries, that for us dated back to before the eighteenth-century UK industrial revolution. Harvest was being collected by scythe and with oxen carts. Spinning wheels were a common sight, and women sat on the floor for hours rolling cigars. They earned just two dollars for each 1,000 cigars rolled.

This view of rural life was a real contrast to the Myanmar I had been shown whilst working in Yangon and Mandalay, and poles apart from Naypyidaw, the pristine administrative capital that replaced Yangon in 2005. All my Ministerial official meetings, both on this first trip and on a subsequent trip to Myanmar, had to be held in Naypyidaw, even though most attendees were Yangon residents.

Naypyidaw, designed by the military regime, is carefully planned and underpopulated, with wide empty roads and enormous unoccupied and very impressive hotels. The most amazing, but for me most uncomfortable site visited whilst wasting time in between official meetings, was to the Naypyidaw gem museum. In a country where officially 25% of the population live in poverty, you enter this vast museum through a room lined and furnished with jade and go through into a warehouse-sized room crammed full of piles of precious gemstones.

The natural wealth of Myanmar was also evident in government buildings. When attending Ministerial meetings, it is impossible not to be impressed by the jewel-encrusted tapestries that adorn the walls.

The Health Ministers, who seem to usually be doctors, have, when I've met them, always been delightful, respectful, helpful, and interested. My very first encounter in 2017 was, however, uncomfortable. Rakhine genocide claims had just been raised.

Before the Minister had even sat down, he asked,

"Professor Ellis what do you think we should do about Rakhine?" Civil service training kicked in.

"Mm so difficult," I calmly replied and rapidly re-directed the conversation back to child health and indeed the need for specialist nursing.

The meeting went well. However, after the customary group photograph, having noticed that although we were discussing nursing no Burmese nurses were present, I asked if I could meet the government senior nurse. There was a lot of muttering in Burmese, but eventually I was escorted into the far scruffier bowels of the building, and shown into a cramped room, where an anxious-looking lady jumped from her chair. After a few minutes translated conversation, having realised I was also a nurse, she became verbose and spent 30 minutes describing the challenges of nursing in Myanmar. In 2019 I met this lady again, and her confidence seemed to have been transformed by involvement in the Nursing Now initiative, a global campaign, initiated in the UK to raise the status and profile of nursing around the world.

Nurses are the largest global health workforce, and I still get excited when, around the world, I meet inspirational nurses striving so hard to improve care. Through all my charity work it has been an honour, and indeed a joy to see what a difference nurses can make, but I also get so frustrated to see how difficult it is for nurses to be heard or even noticed. I have never missed an opportunity to remind people that I am a nurse, but I am realistic that my Professorial title, and various job titles, have probably made global health system leaders more willing to engage in discussions about the value of nursing.

When I have completed my allowed term of office as Chair of THET I already have plans to continue supporting charity projects, including those that will advance the value, impact, and position of nursing around the world. I have worked with enough well-meaning retired professionals to be realistic about the impact I will really be able to make. I want to help others learn from the past but avoid pontificating about what has gone before.

I recognise my strength is now in ensuring charities are effectively governed, not current clinical practice, or new educational approaches. I hope that I can inspire and encourage a younger generation to creatively engage in charity activity.

PART III

STAYING IN FLIGHT

My life is lived at frantic pace
Which make it vital now to trace
How faith in God has been my guide
As I've travelled far and wide,
And through it all you are assured
Health concerns are not ignored.

CHAPTER 10

FAITH

Neither of my parents were practising Christians, but from when I was six, Jane and I, each Sunday, used to take ourselves the mile and a half down to the village United Reformed Church, often cadging a lift home from neighbours. Originally tempted by joining the junior choir, we became stalwarts of the Sunday School, and by the age of twelve I was helping to run the infant section. The church was incredibly welcoming, and particularly child friendly with over a hundred children attending each week. Jane and I became an accepted part of the church family, joining all church activity, and for many years organised the mammoth Christmas party which attracted over two hundred children. Musical Chairs was mayhem!

My family certainly lived by Christian values, but it was at this church that I started to develop my Christian faith. There has never for me been that moment of revelation, just a steady deepening of my faith, and indeed I sometimes feel jealous of those that seem to never doubt or question. What I do know is that without my faith I would have struggled to nurse, particularly when caring for dying children. When I was a ward sister, a parent of one of the children who was dying sent me a poem that he'd written to God, which stated within it, 'tis not for me to understand the complex plan thou hast in hand, but I accept thy will be done, but please take me, don't take my son'. A complex plan indeed when seeing the devastation of devoted parents saying farewell to their children. It was rarely appropriate, at this time of personal loss, to comfort them with my own belief that their child was going to a better place, away from the trials and tribulations of life. I also questioned, and my faith was certainly tested, but I always knew even in bad and sad days that God was with me.

My faith has not only given meaning to my life and my work, but, when I have truly listened and trusted, has guided both my actions and the paths I have taken. This may sound as though my faith means I remain calm and accepting of all of life's knocks. Not true. I am as disappointed, and indeed sometimes as upset and angry as the next man when life seems unfair or is not going how I think it should.

I often appeal to God to show me what he wants from me, to send me in the right direction. There have been numerous occasions when I have been 'approached' to apply for senior nursing positions; Chief Nursing Officer of England; CEO of the International Council of Nurses; CEO of the Royal College of Nursing; and even a seat in the House of Lords. I failed to be appointed to any of them, and there has been the usual problem that, although surprised to be asked, and hesitant to proceed, once I had put effort into understanding the potential role, and spent hours filling in forms or even attending different levels of interviews, I always ended up really wanting to be appointed.

With rejection has come understandable disappointment, and an immediate plummet in self-confidence, but never anger, as in a strange way there has also been a sense of excitement. If not this post, what is God's plan for me? I have longed for clarity, but over time have realised that with each application has come a better understanding of all the organisations that rejected me. This has developed me as a nurse and a health service leader, helping me better function in the roles I have had.

Faith needs continuous commitment, whatever is going on in life. Each evening I randomly read and reflect on passages from the bible, pray for those I love, and thank the Lord for the day. However bad it has been there is always something positive to be thankful for. Each morning I pray for guidance for the day ahead, a routine developed during my Nightingale nurse training.

At the start of the morning shift, all the nurses gathered around the desk, often kneeling, and the most senior student read the morning prayer into a ward microphone. It was a daily reminder that everything we said and did whilst on shift must be for the good of our patients. There was to be no sharing of your personal woes with patients.

The patients were respectful of this brief prayer time. TVs, radios, and buzzers were silent. Patients, whatever their own faith, realised this was an important moment of focus for the staff.

Although I have tried as a Christian to live my life according to the teachings and example of Jesus as God's son, and by God's holy word in the Bible, I respect and am fascinated by other faiths. This fascination was encouraged throughout my childhood, particularly in relation to Judaism. The village had a large reformed Jewish Synagogue which had a familiarisation exchange scheme with the United Reformed Church, and around 20 percent of the girls at Manchester High School for Girls were Jewish.

This understanding of the Jewish faith was invaluable when I became a ward sister in North Manchester, caring for many Orthodox Jewish families. I understood the reason behind Kosher diets and the importance of Jewish festivals, and respectfully ensured all nursing care took account of the Jewish sabbath restrictions. For example, in very practical terms, we made sure that each sabbath the bulbs were removed from the milk fridges so feeds could still be fetched, that Terry rather than disposable nappies were used with a tuck in method rather than safety pins, and no pencils were left in the children's rooms, etc.

For some faiths there was a need to understand why certain, or indeed any medical treatment was unacceptable. One of my best friends at senior school was a Christian Scientist, and on occasions she would ask me to come along to join her on her church outings. All went well until I was asked what career I had chosen, which led to a lecture on the need to reject medical care and truly believe in the power of prayer. This doctrine, a year later, caused a major fall out between my friend's family and the school. My friend was injured at school, and unable to contact her family, the sports teacher accompanied her to hospital where it was found that her wrist was broken. Her arm was put into a Plaster of Paris (PoP) splint. The next day she returned without the PoP. I never really knew if this was my friend's wish or just her complying with her family's direction.

Once nursing I came across similar conflicts between faith and medicine, and the incredible complexity of balancing parental faith and a child's welfare. I learnt that every effort must be made to comply with a family's beliefs and convictions. In the case of Jehovah Witnesses this meant avoiding the administration of blood. I have never recovered from the shock of seeing parents of a young child walk away from their little one, never to return, when the only lifesaving option, and the option reluctantly taken by an A and E consultant, was to give blood. Although devastated for the child and the family in this situation, in a strange way I rather envied the strength of their faith.

As I have worked alongside health service colleagues, and travelled around the world, I have seen so much faith and passion, but what I have also come to recognise is that so many faiths share rules to live by. The ten commandments of Judaism and Christianity reflect the five Buddhists precepts, and when working with Muslim colleagues I have come to recognise and admire each individual's commitment to meeting the obligations of the five pillars of Islam. Indeed, in all faiths I have seen evidence of the desire to live a good and responsible life.

Everywhere I go I seek to understand, and in turn try to help others understand my faith. Justifying my faith and trying to answer others' questions has over time strengthened my own faith as a Christian. On my last working trip to Myanmar, a young Burmese colleague and I had a spare hour between two appointments, and on exiting Yangon hospital and walking towards a coffee shop, she pointed out Holy Trinity Anglican Cathedral. I asked if she had ever been into a Christian church. She sheepishly said no but she would like to. We risked life and limb to cross the main road, and it was then I noticed the barbed wire and barriers around the building. Not to be deterred, we entered by a partially opened gate, and then finding the door firmly locked, but hearing voices, we walked around the building. Two workmen looked a bit staggered to see us. When I asked if we could enter, they indicated a large open window. The church was definitely in need of renovation, but simplistically beautiful, and certainly a total contrast to Myanmar's ornate Buddhist temples. Sitting on a pew, I felt as though I'd gone back to pre-reformation time, using the statues and windows to try and tell my young colleague about Jesus and Christian beliefs. I am not sure at the end of the half hour I had not confused rather than educated her. This was not helped when on leaving the Anglican church we passed Catholic, Baptist, and Methodist churches and she asked me to explain the differences! I made a rudimentary attempt to respond.

I admit that I find defending my own faith difficult when I am also trying to show respect to others. This was particularly true when I was on holiday with friends, and we decided, having explored some Utah and Nevada National Parks, to fly from Salt Lake City to Washington DC. I am not sure that I had even considered that this would provide us with an opportunity to learn more about the Mormons. My pre-existent knowledge was embarrassingly based upon a childhood crush on the Osmonds, a trip to see 'The Book of

Mormon' musical at a London theatre, and driving past the UK Mormon temple near my north-west home.

Arriving in Salt Lake City on a sunny day we were stunned by the gleaming white beauty of the iconic buildings. We joined tours of Brigham Young's house and the limited public areas of the Mormon Temple. Our eager young guides were certainly enthusiastic, but this made us strangely reluctant to ask questions that may embarrass or offend them.

The next morning, having unashamedly restored our caffeine levels in the hotel, we set off to tour the very impressive 21,000-capacity Church of Jesus Christ of Latter-Day Saints Conference Centre. When we entered, we were relieved when our allocated guide, Ray, turned out to be a delightful, chatty, 75-year-old.

Ray spent three hours showing us the building, sharing his life story, and explaining the beliefs, traditions, and modern-day practices of the Church of Jesus Christ of Latter-Day Saints. He not only encouraged us to ask questions, but obviously enjoyed the lively exchanges. He showed no sign of embarrassment or doubt. When asked why the church could not produce the golden plates, the source from which Joseph Smith translated the Book of Mormon, he said with a twinkle in his eye,

"You're not going to like this. They have returned to God so no one can gain from their existence, and as a test of our faith."

When I asked why the Quorum of Apostles, the church leaders, were all men, he laughed. "You sound like my wife and daughter," he said.

The morning ended with an opportunity to actually read some of the Book of Mormon, which was in style very like reading the Old Testament.

I left Salt Lake City unconvinced, but certainly far better informed, and, in a way, more respectful. I expect non-believers not to ridicule my Christian beliefs, some of which they may find farfetched. The Mormons deserved the same courtesy.

My Christian beliefs have stood firm, but at different times in my life I have enjoyed and benefited from different approaches to Christian worship. I admit that I have never been very 'happy clappy'. The more complex and chaotic my life has become, and wherever in the world I have found myself, I have appreciated the consistency and familiarity of the Anglican churches' traditions.

Although services are comfortingly similar, it has been a fascination to see how Anglican services are adapted in different countries, and in response to different social and economic times. For example, in Uganda, at the height of the HIV/AIDS epidemic, the reading of bands of marriage for each prospective couple took about 20 minutes. The need to declare any other sexual partners was repeatedly demanded, to the point that even we began to feel guilty!

To work in these countries, I have realised that you have to be realistic and handle the fact that some national and local beliefs are unacceptable, or actually abhorrent to our Western sensitivities. Examples would be the vilification of homosexuality, or genocide of religious groups. It is moments like these that I am, and I convince myself necessarily, cowardly. I avoid discussing contentious topics, determinedly focusing on the development of the health care workforce and the improvement of health and health care.

Even within Christian countries and at home, there are challenges to accepting others' beliefs. I have many Catholic friends and I struggle with the element of fear, obedience, and guilt some Catholic doctrine seems to engender. This is so opposite to my faith and belief in a loving and forgiving God. This was reinforced one year when, due to a shortage of registered nurse volunteers, I and my friend Frances, who is also an Anglican, were cajoled into joining a pilgrimage to Lourdes.

I could easily accept the positive impact of the pilgrimage on our adult patients, who gained great comfort and indeed peace from visiting the grotto and taking the water. I was not as sold on the experience when I witnessed the desperation of parents of a terminally ill four-year-old, who each evening could be found pleading at the grotto for their son to be cured.

The expectation from all was that because Frances and I were there, we were Catholic. Patients literally recoiled when we informed them that we would not be attending mass as we were not Catholic. Then one night, whilst off duty in the pub, we were informed quite openly by a priest, who had certainly consumed too much wine, that as Anglicans we would not be going to heaven. This statement was followed up with a lecture on how we had been damned by the exploits of Henry VIII, and why we should pray to the saints, not directly to God! On the last night, we were told that it is tradition to walk clockwise three times around a statue of Our Lady of Lourdes, as this guarantee's returning to Lourdes one day. We walked anticlockwise and it worked. I have never returned.

With my Christian faith has come long-lasting friendships with members of local and global church communities. When in Uganda I still go to the St Paul's Anglican Cathedral to meet my friend Jessica. When living alone and holding senior positions in London, Sunday at church was my time of inspiration, succour, and peace. Then, after the church service, I could unwind over coffee, or a glass of wine, knowing I was safely in the company of fellow Christians, even benefiting from a few hugs. Leaving this London church family was the hardest retirement decision I had to take, but I underestimated the welcome at the local village church. The choir welcomed a hesitant alto, and I am following yet another new path as a Governor of the village school.

I continue to rely on my Christian faith to meet life's challenges.

CHAPTER 11

HOLIDAYS

Holidays have always been an integral part of my life. A time to relax with family and friends. A vital opportunity to explore; to step away from the realities of day-to-day life; regroup, recharge, and return refreshed.

During my childhood, with both parents full time working, the main family bonding time was the annual family holiday, always to somewhere hot in Europe. Dad was certainly a sun worshipper, with an impressive collection of very brief swimming attire, and a willingness to bare all on nudist beaches, much to my mother's chagrin.

As a young child, as holiday departure dates loomed, I begged to stay at home with my grandmother as holidays were no joy. I was fair skinned and always got sunburnt, and eating foreign food invariably gave me the 'squits'. However, the family holiday was sacrosanct as it was the most consistent time we spent together as a family.

Mum in those early years would not fly, and the drives, usually to the Mediterranean, in a far from reliable car were an endurance test, but an opportunity for Dad to use his fluent French and patchy Spanish. Finances were tight. I have memories of running out of money for petrol on the drive home, but this annual pilgrimage to foreign parts, which was rare in the 1960s, now brings back some great memories.

As a child, our annual holiday to North Wales was, for me, far more enjoyable, and in 1971, Mum and Dad, having been left a small inheritance, purchased a terraced miner's cottage in Trefor, near Caernarfon. This was for many years our weekend bolt hole. It allowed Dad the opportunity to obtain solitude on long walks, or in later years to benefit from the efforts of the Royal National Lifeboat Institute. They were regularly called upon to rescue him as he uncontrollably headed out to sea on his windsurfer.

Mum seemed to spend most of her time at the cottage cleaning, clearing blocked drains and chatting to neighbours. Her friendliness, and perhaps our Welsh-sounding but actually Yorkshire surname, Ellis, seemed to make us well accepted by the villagers. This was important, as in the 1970s the Meibion Glyndwr ('sons of Glyndŵr') Welsh Nationalist movement were torching holiday homes.

In the late 1970s and early 1980s when I was a poor Nurse student, the cottage became a great place to share with my equally impoverished friends. Christmas at the cottage was certainly different. The day started with the local prize-winning brass band weaving their way through each terraced house; in the front door out the back; in the back, out the front. It certainly discouraged any thought of a Christmas morning lie in.

The cottage was sold in 1995, by which time Mum was a little weary with her cottage maintenance duties, and we were using the cottage less and less. We could all now afford holidays to countries where the weather was a little more reliable. I had started my lifelong habit of visiting countries far and wide, and my parents were accompanying Jane and her young family on biannual beach holidays. This, however, did not stop Jane and me grasping opportunities to holiday together, a formula we knew worked.

Our first 'sisters together' trip was when I was 15 and Jane 19. We booked a package holiday to Italy, the first of our many lifetime visits to Florence, Rome, and Venice. All went well until the attempted return flight from Milan. Sitting watching our plane being loaded it was suddenly engulfed in flames! A little unnerving, and 24 hours later some passengers refused to board the replacement flight. We never considered this option, particularly after a fellow passenger shared his excess duty-free spirit allowance with us! Our biggest concern, and challenge, was contacting Mum and Dad. There were no mobile phones in 1975, and in Italy at the time, low denomination coins were very scarce. This made making a phone call almost impossible. Jane managed to cadge a few coins from a shop assistant, but only enough to say to Mum, before being cut off, "Our plane has gone up in flames—"

Not a reassuring message, and when we arrived at Manchester Airport, my Dad was there anxiously waiting, having camped out in the arrivals area for over 24 hours. I think, with the confidence of youth at 15, I only really appreciated how scary this must have been for my parents when I saw the relief on his face, and Mum's tears when we walked in the front door.

It was many years before we were allowed to holiday together again, but shared trips have continued throughout our adult years. Indeed, some of my most amusing memories have been when travelling with Jane, probably as she is willing to take risks and likes nothing more than sourcing unusual destinations.

One such holiday followed Jane's attendance at a conference in Brisbane. We decided to take the opportunity to visit Lady Elliot Island and the barrier reef. They were both stunning, but the most memorable highlight of this particular trip was a visit to Fraser Island. Fraser Island is renowned for its beauty as the world's largest 'sand' island, a fact that became all too real. We hired the required four-wheel drive vehicle, having never driven one before. Sadly within 10 minutes of disembarking from the ferry we were totally bogged down in sand, unaware that due to two year's drought the islands sand roads were considered virtually impassable!

The car's instruction manual made the helpful suggestion of placing sticks and leaves beneath the wheels, which I was tackling with vigour until the Australian manual foot note reminded the stranded motorist to be aware of deadly snakes and insects whilst gathering from Australian woodland. In desperation the towels and snorkelling flippers were deployed, and we progressed for a further mile before again sinking deep into the sand road. The relief of spying an approaching ranger was soon dashed when he refused to assist, stating tourists in distress were not his business. Our fear of abandonment was lifted when a group of eager macho Australian young men physically lifted our vehicle back onto terra firma.

Five more miles and we were stranded again, and this time a very helpful Australian couple offered assistance. Dropping the tyre pressure to aid grip, and then deploying a snap rope (an ingenious stretching tow rope that having been expanded jerks the car from the sand) they not only got us moving but also provided us with strict instructions about sand-driving techniques and passable roads. It was a great relief to arrive at our beach-side chalet, one of four, but many miles from the nearest town or shop. On reviewing our supplies – one packet of rich tea biscuits, one steak, but two bottles of Australian wine – we decided shopping was not essential. The apartment was in the most beautiful position, overlooking 75-mile beach, which is stated on the culture trip website as 'the most dangerous beach in the world', known for the large number of 'dingo attacks', 'saltwater crocodiles,' and the 'favourite hangout for young Great White sharks.' We innocently walked along the beach, and on the nearest headland, spied to our surprise and delight the conservatory of a pub. Having ensconced ourselves on two very comfortable chairs overlooking the sea view, we awaited service. When a man approached, we did not hesitate to order two large gin and tonics. The 'waiter' looked a little surprised, and to our total embarrassment responded, "You're more than welcome to a G and T, ladies, but this is actually my lounge." We apologised profusely but the G and T's were excellent!

On the return to our chalet, we considered how to prepare our one steak. The only cooking facility was an outdoor barbecue, and, whilst we were reviewing the lighting instructions, the neighbours returned from a fishing trip. On enquiring if we had a problem, we admitted we had never lit a barbecue. They immediately offered to throw our meagre offering onto their 'barbie' with their day's catch, in return for watching an Australian Football League match on our chalet's TV. It was the only TV in the area. Jane and I had a great evening with the two wives consuming the wine and nibbling Rich Tea biscuits.

Waking in the morning a new challenge was ahead. We now had to drive down 75- mile beach to reach the ferry back to the mainland, but there were a number of hazards. There was a three-hour slot when the tide was out and the sand hard enough to drive on. Light aircraft used the beach as a runway during the same three-hour slot, and at regular intervals there were deep run-in channels to be navigated. A drive we never wish to repeat.

Anxiety reached its peak one mile from the ferry dock. The tide was now coming in and a large tree had fallen across the beach 'road', so the only way past was to drive in and out of the sea between waves! I counted and Jane drove, ignoring the hire car restrictions for not driving on a beach, or in sea water! On arrival at the ferry, totally exhausted, a kindly Australian manoeuvred the car into position, and we celebrated driving off onto tarmac!

This certainly was not the only 'interesting' situation Jane and I found ourselves in on our shared overseas jaunts. In 1995 Johannesburg was another memorable trip. This time it was one of my work trips. I was there to chair one day of a three-day African Continents Nurse Managers conference, after which we had booked a safari to Madikwe Game Park.

On arrival, we discovered that thousands of South African nurses at state-funded hospitals had just gone on strike, demanding increased salaries. Nurse Manager's had been recalled, so chairing of the three days was now in my hands. It was a brilliant experience but exhausting.

Delegates, bedecked in their colourful National Dress, were all so eager. There were almost fights to volunteer to be included in role play, and if group work was initiated the cacophony of multi-language chatter was deafening. I had never before, and have never again, chaired a conference where the audience refused to take breaks, or wanted to continue long after finish times. Even at breakfast, when I was hoping for time to gather my thoughts, Jane and my table for two soon found itself as a base for at least six as chairs were dragged up to join us.

On the last day, the local delegates proudly announced that for my one free afternoon before departing on our safari, they had arranged a Soweto tour for us. It was fascinating.

Starting in wealthy Soweto, where Winnie Mandela lived, we were taken by David, our guide, to see each economic level of Soweto housing. As a regular visitor to Uganda, I was not too shocked by the living conditions we saw, but the size of Soweto was staggering, with over one and a half million population crammed into the 32 townships.

The most heart-breaking visit of the day was to the Hector Pieterson Memorial and Museum, named after a 12-year-old who was killed alongside 170 other school children in the Anti-Apartheid

Soweto uprising in June 1976.

We came out of the museum feeling dazed and sad, but our spirits were to be lifted by a group of about 30 immaculately clad young children from a Soweto school who were standing on the memorial steps, passionately singing the South African National Anthem.

After about two hours of the tour Jane, now in the front seat next to David and attempting to chatter, asked the memorable question,

"Do you have trouble with gangs? We do in the cities in the UK."

His reply, "Oh no. We call them in and say 'you are very naughty boys. This must stop.' Three months later we call them in again and if they have not stopped, we shoot them."

"Blimey, what do the police say?" Jane spluttered.

"The police?" he said, looking confused. "This is Soweto."

We wanted to think David was trying to shock us, but this information rang true when we met a doctor at the Chris Hani Baragwanath (Bara) Hospital who informed us that he saw around 160 gunshot victims a month.

The Bara hospital was quite a sight. The largest hospital in Africa, and third largest hospital in the world with around 400 A and E admissions a day. The hospital, reached from Soweto by walking across a road bridge over a busy main road, was in turmoil the day we visited, as strikers had blocked the bridge, threatening the families of any staff trying to cross.

Jane and I left for Madikwe in a hire car with safety warnings ringing in our ears; 'Don't stop at traffic lights but crawl slowly forward until the lights change'; 'Be careful not to have maps or tourist items on show'; 'Don't stop for petrol'. The journey was uneventful, and our only tense moment was once we entered Madikwe. The road was blocked by five grumpy-looking elephants!

We returned to South Africa again when Jane attended a conference in Cape Town. This gave us not only the chance to appreciate the stunning beauty of the garden route, but to also once more immerse ourselves in the apartheid history of the Country. Visits to Robben Island and the Apartheid Museum were eye opening, but the most personally challenging was seeing, as we travelled, the disparity of wealth and lifestyles. Visiting South Africa required uncomfortable honest reflection. I had the nerve to condemn the obvious poverty of the townships as we drove through on our way to be pampered in five-star accommodation.

Travelling with Jane does usually involve 'posh' accommodation, but sometimes our plans are thwarted by actual availability. This was true when she accompanied me to Uganda in 2015. For the first time on a Uganda visit, I organised what was supposed to be a luxury holiday to see Murchison Falls. Murchison Falls National Park sits on the shore of Lake Albert, in north-west Uganda, and the falls are where the Victoria Nile River surges through a narrow gap over a massive drop. It is spectacular.

Unlike a visit to Niagara Falls, which is swamped with eager tourists, we were totally alone at Murchison. We wondered if this lack of visitors was because of abduction concerns in the area, or perhaps because of personal safety at the falls. There was certainly no barrier, just a rusty sign precariously perched on the edge of the 400-foot drop which ironically read, 'Please do not go beyond this point!'

We were to discover that the probable reason for the emptiness was simply that it was the rainy season. This certainly made the falls even more impressive, but the rather basic accommodation was cold and very damp, and the roads almost impassable. For some sections of road, the driver paid a local to walk ahead through the floods to confirm that the car would make it!

This was not the only time in my travels I was taken unaware by flooding. In March 2006, I was invited to speak at an International Conference in Darwin. I was accompanied by a colleague and friend from Great Ormond Street Hospital, and we were joined by an Australian friend, a fellow Nightingale. On arriving at Darwin airport, we went to collect our hire car. We were sent out to find our car in bay 64 and stopped, stunned, when before our eyes was a beast of a vehicle; a high riding 4x4 with an impressive exhaust snorkel. Even getting into it was a challenge, requiring a helpful bottom shove. Hesitant at first, once we left Darwin to travel the 150 miles east to visit Kakadu National Park, we realised that this vehicle was to be a life saver.

March is the end of the wet season. The roads were rivers. Fords that we had to cross were raging torrents, with the added crocodile warning signs adding to our sense of unease. Kakadu is described in tourist guides as 'inhospitable' at any time, but particularly in the wet season. Crocodiles can freely move into new and unexpected areas, and the rain fills snakes' habitats with water, forcing them to the surface and to the scarce dry areas where humans are walking. We were told to be particularly wary of the inland taipan or 'fierce snakes', which have the most toxic venom of any terrestrial snake in the world, and which have the 'self-confidence', when they sense humans approaching, to seek and attack. Many paths were closed for safety, but the owner of our guest house suggested that we joined the nightly pilgrimage to Nourlangie Rock to watch the sunset.

We were comforted to realise that this was a popular tourist event and walked with relative confidence through the undergrowth, eventually climbing a vast rock for a good view. It was spectacular, but this excursion became memorable not for its beauty, but because as night fell, and people started scrambling off the rock for the return walk, we realised our stupidity. The clue we had failed to pick up on was in the description 'sunset'. We had never thought to bring a torch! We stumbled along trying to keep other tourists' lights in sight, speeding up with every leaf rustle or perceived movement in the undergrowth. Terrifying!

It was in a way a relief to return to Darwin for the conference, although still hazardous. It was baking hot (38 degrees centigrade) and unpleasantly humid, with no chance to cool off by swimming. The sea had saltwater crocodiles, and the morning we aimed to swim in the hotel pool it was closed to allow them to remove a crocodile that had wandered in overnight. The disgruntled Australian delegates questioned why the conference had been held in Darwin, but for us it was a unique opportunity and an experience we would have been sorry to miss.

Holidays for me should be full of new sights and sounds, new experiences, and I have been joined in my global adventures by various friends. During nurse training the deciding factor for our choice was cost. We stayed in some very dodgy digs in Greece and Turkey, ambiguously advertised as 'village rooms'.

As money became more available, and as I became braver, my travels took me further afield. In 1982, I and a nursing friend from Manchester, Anne, travelled to India. It was on this trip that I probably first discovered my fascination with other cultures, and the enjoyment I got from mixing with locals. Staying within the safe confines of a hotel or lying for hours on a beach is not for me.

Having found willing companions, my holiday exploits have taken me right around the world, with so many beautiful destinations etched forever in my memories. Australia and the USA have been regular and the most relaxing destinations. This is probably because they are English speaking, with a reliable health service, and in each I have good friends to offer advice on the best and safest places to visit in these enormous countries. The most memorable destinations have, however, been those where experiences have been more 'unusual', or just a little more daunting!

Nepal was one such destination. An absolutely fascinating country, and in March 2011, I and my three friends felt honoured to visit. In the first few days we aimlessly wandered around Kathmandu, soaking in the pleasant atmosphere and frequently commenting of the beauty of not only the numerous sights, but also of the people. On the fourth day, we had booked a sunrise flight around Everest. Setting off from the hotel at five a.m., all was quiet. The flight was amazing, with the clearest views of Everest against a deep blue sky. We landed full of excitement for the day ahead, only to be told that we were now stuck at the airport due to fuel riots across the city. Violent protesters were refusing to let any vehicles drive on the roads. After a two hour wait, one of our group, Liz, convinced the driver to drape a tourist flag across the front of the vehicle, and to try getting us back to the hotel. The guide was terrified and hid under the back seat of the minibus. Liz, a grey-haired respectable English lady, joined the driver, taking the front passenger seat. The three of us sat in clear view at every window, and we set off. Almost immediately we came across a roadblock of burning tyres, and as we approached around 20 protesters brandishing sticks and bricks ran towards the now stationary vehicle. The driver shook and Liz, as calm as a cucumber, lowered the passenger window, leant out, smiled, and extended her hand to the first protester, saying, "Good morning. So lovely to meet you. This is such a beautiful country. We are delighted to be here."

Totally bemused, the protester stopped dead in his tracks, dropped the brick, and shook her hand, bowing as he did so. We then all started waving and smiling at the other protesters, and they waved back as we slowly crawled through the roadblock. This surreal performance was repeated three more times before we swept into the hotel car park, and a shaking guide crawled out from his hiding place.

That afternoon we walked around the city with no concerns for our safety. When we realised that we were totally lost, we were not surprised that a kindly Nepalese man walked us safely back to the hotel, refusing any recompense beyond being able to practice his English.

On return home from this trip, we were busy showing people the wonderful photos when we read that, on September 25th, 2011, Flight 103, the same Everest tourist flight we had taken, had crashed, killing all 19 people on board. Then, on April 25th, 2015, my Nepal photos became even more special and distressing. The Nepal Gorkha earthquake had that day killed around 9,000 and destroyed 600,000 structures around Kathmandu.

Global travel certainly reminds you of the awesome force of nature. This was not the first time earthquakes had transformed landscapes that I had enjoyed. In 1989 the San Francisco earthquake destroyed the beautiful buildings of Pier 39 Fisherman's Wharf that I had so admired when I first visited in 1979, and in 2011 the beautiful Christchurch Cathedral, and the Novotel hotel we had stayed in, in 2005, were devastated by the New Zealand earthquake.

Coming from our safe little island, where our greatest natural risk is flooding, hearing of the horrific life-threatening impact of extreme natural disasters, such as earthquakes, always begs the question, 'why would anyone choose to live there?' I certainly think this every time I visit places in the shadow of smoking volcanoes, like Vesuvius and Etna. I can never decide if this is because those at risk are in denial, have no option, or are just fatalistic.

Destructive volcano eruptions are rare, but the risk of having all your worldly goods destroyed by fire is, in some places I have visited, almost guaranteed. I realised how much value I put on 'belongings' when chatting to a tour guide in South East Australia. He described to me the meagre contents of the fireproof boxes that he and his wife keep in their cars in fire season, knowing it may be all they can save. This family's whole outlook was so different from ours in the UK, where protection of property is paramount. Our guide's wife apparently spent many happy hours choosing, from a catalogue, the next wooden house she would put on the burnt-out plot.

This couple accepted fire loss as essential for natural regeneration of their unique Australian habitat, and I saw similar acceptance in Tasmania in 2013 and in Athens in 2008.

Danger from natural disaster just has to be accepted when travelling. Man-made danger that leads to a change of holiday plans, is far harder to take.

In Africa, political unrest is the usual trigger for a rapid exit. At the end of my first Kenyan safari in 2005, a few days stay in Nairobi was curtailed when a referendum between 'Orange' and 'Banana' supporters became violent. Great names for political parties! The strange twist was that, for our safety, we flew immediately into Uganda, where we always travelled with an armed policeman.

Offered protection, I always accept as I have never been one to take unnecessary risks. This includes travelling with an extensive health kit, even if in developed countries, and I have every suggested pre-departure immunisation, and conscientiously take anti-malarial drugs. I have to own up to also carrying an emergency broad spectrum course of antibiotics and loads of Loperamide (medicine to treat diarrhoea). You never know which unusual delicacy will trigger a stomach upset, and I like to try every food type on offer.

Holidays are not enjoyable if you feel unwell, and I do enjoy my holidays, well most of them!

The only holiday I wished I had never gone on was a cruise. Having been attracted by the thought of being able to unpack just once, and yet still awake each day in a new destination, Kathy and I, in 2002, booked a Mediterranean cruise. I hated everything about it! Being trapped on a ship or invading picturesque ports with over three and a half thousand people, was a nightmare. Adverts, filmed when quiet, did not correctly portray the constant queuing, failure to find seats where you actually wanted to sit, and the enforced socialisation.

This was particularly true at mealtimes when, as a party of two, we were instructed to sit with six other people we didn't know, and we soon found out that we really didn't want to know. The mealtime conversation always commenced with, "Where have you cruised before?"

This was a brief conversation being our first cruise.

One of the most aggravating cruise exchanges I entered into was with an American at our dinner table, who, on discovering we were English, asked in a New York drawl, "Do you have cows?"

Thinking I had misheard I politely said, "Pardon?"

With which she responded, "COWS, moo, moo."

I acquiesced and, not to be halted she asked, "What language do you talk in England?"

"English, unlike you," I witheringly responded.

From that moment on I decided I could not survive a week table-sharing. When we reported for dinner that night, I asked the Maître d for a table for two. He politely informed me that they were reserved for honeymoon couples. I did debate saying Kathy and I were a new happy couple, but then inspiration hit. Kathy, whose hearing isn't great, had not heard his response, and I had turned to explain his refusal to her. Turning back, I gently touched his arm, and in a confidential tone whispered, "I am sorry we have to have a table for two as my friend has hearing loss and finds it totally isolating on a larger table."

For the rest of that trip we had a very pleasant table for two.

On our return I vowed never to cruise again but was to be tempted back for a cruise to Alaska. This was far better as we travelled as a foursome, and I had to accept that the only way to really see Alaska is by sea!

Glaciers crashing into the sea certainly increased feelings of guilt about my carbon footprint, but I have to be honest that there are still many areas of the world I hope that I will visit. My travel days are far from over.

CHAPTER 12

HEALTH

My grandmother and mother were avid shoppers. Each Saturday morning I was expected to eagerly accompany them. I was, as a young child, a disappointment as most weeks I would decide after a very short time that I didn't feel well and wanted to go home. I now think that, rather than just being awkward, this was probably the first signs of migraines that have gone on to plague my whole life. As a family, sickness was not encouraged, or even really 'allowed'. If Jane or I awoke feeling rough, the phrase from Mum was always, "Get to school and see how it goes, you can always come home."

I cannot remember ever actually being allowed to come home, but just spending some time in the darkened sick room bed with a vomit bowl.

Living a life with migraines I have become an expert at not only tidy, but timely, vomiting! I can judge when to have a break when Chairing meetings to allow me to retreat to a bathroom and to give enough time for migraine injections to take effect. I've spent some time locked in toilets in the House of Commons, numerous hospitals, universities, and in airports and hotels all around the world. I have perfected the art of injecting into my leg without exposing myself in public places, Euston Station being a regular venue.

My nearest and dearest friends and family can spot that I am suffering, but I don't bleat on about having migraines. There are far worse conditions to have, and I have made it a mission not to let migraines rule or ruin my life, or to let them define who I am.

This came home to me when Anne and I, whilst on a holiday in Venezuela, met an English couple.

"I'm June. I don't work because I get migraines," was the wife's introductory statement. Then, much to the obvious embarrassment of her husband, she proceeded to empty out her handbag to show us the tablets she always had to carry, just in case she felt a migraine coming on.

Unlike June I have made sure that people I meet, and most colleagues, do not know I'm a migraine sufferer. I have had a need-to-know approach. My secretaries have known that if I say 'just give me 20 minutes' it means I need to vomit, inject, and recover before continuing the day's activities. On rare occasions a taxi home has been required.

The most difficult jobs to hold down as a migraine sufferer were my earlier clinical roles. I could not just reorganise or delay my day's activities. The patients' care could not wait, and I was often the only registered nurse on duty. I have vivid memories of explaining to parents why I entered a cubicle to give their child IV drugs, gripping a 'just in case' vomit bowl.

The more senior my roles, the easier it has been to rearrange the diary or delegate. It is a good lesson for personal humility to learn that no one is irreplaceable. There was one particularly notable day when I was Director of Nursing at GOSH. I had staggered in because, after months of preparation, the government inspectors were due to visit. Finding me stooped over a toilet, my Deputy dispatched me home. The visit went well, and it gave individuals who had actually done the preparatory work the opportunity to shine.

Over the years I've tried every approach to control and manage migraine episodes, from conventional drug therapy to alternative therapies, and even wacky suggestions. I've been injected or needled in various places, worn magnets, drunk herbal drinks, and been on very restrictive diets. A three-week American holiday on a ketogenic (no sugars or carbohydrate) diet was certainly a challenge. American eateries were incapable of serving breakfast without hash browns, or Caesar salads without croutons. My 'side of the plate' crouton wall building abilities became a regular activity. The diet didn't make a sustainable difference to my migraines but was a welcome boost to my constant battle against obesity! After six months, with great relief I returned to a normal diet, and the slimming clubs, but still with unresolved migraine attacks.

What I unhealthily found was that, if I worked at top pace, limited deep sleep, and started my day before six a.m., the number of migraines that impacted on my work reduced. It was wind down time that mainly caused problems. Each week Saturday was a write off, and every holiday had to have an initial three-day buffer before activities started.

Over the years, the side effects of preventative drugs proved to be, on balance, more limiting to life than the migraines themselves. This was particularly true of anti-epilepsy drugs which interfered with my ability to think, reason, and remember my cognitive ability. With one drug, it reached the point where I was repeating sentences when writing reports or letters, and I became so indecisive that I couldn't even manage to food shop. Certainly not my norm.

I was working at GOSH and in spite of superb support from my Deputy, Janet, others started to notice, including the CEO. She contacted the Medical Director of the National Neurological Hospital. I had never before used my professional background to facilitate access to NHS services, but I could not have been more grateful when I received an appointment within a week. I cannot imagine how I could have continued working if I had had to join the NHS two-year migraine clinic waiting list. The preventative epilepsy drugs were stopped and my mind cleared. The National Hospital team have been my support network ever since.

My migraines are now treated by injection as they occur and kept controllable with three monthly Botox injections. One of my nieces finds it amusing to drop into conversation that her Aunt has regular Botox. The hearer looks incredulous when inspecting my age-lined face, obviously feeling I am wasting my money. Botox has only been available on the NHS for about two years, and my treatment did cost me a lot for over eight years. It has been worth every penny as it has made living with migraines manageable, but I have had to accept that migraines are with me for life. They are part of who I am and dictate how I live.

I have not allowed them to restrict me, but they have definitely made me better pace my frantic life, enforcing down time. They were certainly one of the reasons for my early retirement from paid employment. I recognised that my migraines were becoming less controllable and more exhausting as I tried to continue working at full throttle, as well as increasing my commitment to voluntary global health activity. I needed to slow down so that I could really enjoy life to the full, for as long as possible. There is always that niggling concern that with migraines comes a near-doubling of the risk of ischaemic stroke.

I was also keen to give up paid work before I potentially succumbed to dementia, a devastating condition I had encountered throughout my life, and a 30% increased possibility for me due to family history.

In 1978, a few days into my first ward placement in London, there was the wailing sound of air raid sirens. The frail elderly gentleman I was with, paled, grabbed my arm and, with incredible strength, dragged me under the bed. This was my first encounter with dementia. No amount of rational explanation that this was merely a test of the London imminent flood warning system could convince George that either of us were safe to emerge. So, under the bed we sat until the sister's head appeared, reassuring us the 'all clear' had sounded. George's preoccupation with the war continued, and we regularly had to 'bail out over Germany' before he would agree that it was safe to have a wash.

The elderly relatives I had been around as a child had all been totally compos mentis, and although I had met occasional patients like George, and worked in a specific EMI (Elderly Mentally Infirm) unit as part of my nurse training, I never envisaged that dementia would have such a profound impact on my life. Dementia was to effect both my parents.

It would be easy, but I think probably unhelpful, to depressingly recount observing my parents' sad decline. Yes, we saw in my mother the early frustration and fear as her mental function declined, and we cried when observing the later total dependence of this vibrant lady. We watched my father, the gentlest and kindest person, become angry and aggressive. These were indeed difficult times to live through, but as the years pass the family increasingly recount the good times before dementia, and even some of the amusing facets of my parents' behaviour that made us laugh when all seemed so unbearable.

In the early days it was simple acts that we could all laugh at together. My mother was staggered when the phone wouldn't work when she had just decided to wash it in a bowl of soapy water. None of us could understand why their television kept changing to Japanese, a reset that Jane and I could never replicate. Carers were never allowed to clean, but encouraged to sit and chat, and share a cup of tea rather than prepare food.

Jane, as the local living daughter, was phenomenal. She constantly checked on them and made sure they were safe and cared for. I just felt useless, and at one point applied for a Nurse Directors position that would allow me to move to the hospital near my parents.

After the interview I was not offered the post as the panel felt I was 'overqualified and would be bored and not stay.' I was furious at the time, but they were probably right. I returned to London life, visiting the North once or twice a month.

Mum and Dad loved London, but as their dementia worsened visits to see me became more and more hazardous. They seemed to be totally unaware of any danger. If, whilst I was at work, they left my flat, they just couldn't find their way back. One day, during a visit, I got called out of a GOSH Board meeting to collect them from the reception area. They had got lost going to a book shop a hundred yards from my flat. Totally unconcerned they had hailed a taxi, asking for, "A hospital that looks after lots of children."

Thank goodness for helpful London cabbies. It had become clear visiting me was to be a thing of the past, and over time any outing became perilous.

As their memories faded, we regularly found the car missing. They had driven into town, but then forgotten and walked home. We became experts at searching local car parks to retrieve the car and paid numerous overnight parking fees. On one occasion, when Jane and the family were away, and I was theoretically in charge although over 200 miles away, I received a scary phone call from one of their neighbours. My parents and car had disappeared for over 24 hours. I immediately mobilised friends to search the local area, and I headed North. I searched for two days, frantic with worry, and was just so relieved when they calmly walked in as though they had just popped out. Not wanting to scare them, I gently questioned where they had been, but they just look confused and never elucidated. Their whereabouts will always remain a mystery with our only clue a petrol receipt from a garage in Wales!

It was after this that we tried to stop my father driving, concerned not just for their own, but also others safety. The GP refused to help as they had not had an accident and when he had asked my Dad, "Do you enjoy driving?"

"I love it and am an excellent driver," was Dad's reply.

Dad's decline brought with it some unexpected behaviour, but the most surprising was when my father insisted on wearing my mother's clothing, particularly her frilly nighties. He had always been a snazzy dresser, and perhaps in a different time would have been a cross dresser. Helen, my eldest niece, who worshipped her grandparents, on arriving and finding Dad in a very flowery puffed sleeve shirt, came out with the memorable statement,

"Oh, very smart. Not many men can carry of a puff sleeve as well as you." None of us cared what he wore, as long as he and my mother were happy.

For a few years the two of them merrily muddled through, but it became increasingly difficult to be really sure that they were safe. We would arrive to find them out, goodness knows where, and they returned in totally unsuitable clothing for the weather. Food prepared by Jane and carers was not eaten, and we found hidden stores of bank notes everywhere. My mother also seemed to be sending money to a number of fraudsters, and on one occasion Jane returned from holiday to find that they had been duped into signing for unneeded double glazing.

In December 2007, Jane and her family were taking a well-deserved holiday to Australia, and as carers were also on holiday, I arranged leave to spend the two weeks with my parents. I had thought that on my fortnightly weekend stays I had got a grasp on how bad things had become. This Christmas visit was to be a real eye opener. Each day a copious amount of fraudulent mail fell on the mat, seeking various monetary payments. The scariest was a threatening demand note from a fortune teller, who had obviously received previous payments from my mother, and which on this occasion stated that Mum's daughters, Jane and I, would be forever cursed if money wasn't immediately sent to a Swiss address. Although my mother had gone beyond being able to respond, this and all other demands were speedily filed in the bin.

If I nipped out for, for example, a pint of milk, I never knew if I would return to an empty flat, which would be followed by an anxious wait to see if they returned safely. I stopped going anywhere without taking them with me, which was a prolonged excursion, as before leaving I had to make sure they were dressed appropriately. Dad would insist that summer shorts were ideal for the minus four degrees temperatures, and Mum seemed to just pile everything on top of her nightwear, sometimes achieving four-outfit layering.

Sleep was also disturbed as the concept of night and day seemed to have deserted them. I would find them both up and dressed in the lounge in the early hours.

A friend of mine joined us for Christmas Day, nobly suffering with me the repeated viewing of the 'Walk of the Penguins' film, that someone had 'thoughtfully' given Dad for Christmas. Those Penguins walked thousands of miles on our TV that day!

Preparing food that Christmas was my relaxation, and whilst I was there, convincing them to eat at mealtimes was no problem. Dad had always enjoyed his food and Mum particularly loved sweet things. However, it became apparent at the end of that visit that they could no longer be relied upon to eat the food that carers prepared and left for them. I returned to work in London on a Sunday afternoon, and when Jane checked on them on the Monday morning, she found the sandwiches and cakes I had left for their Sunday tea untouched, and no evidence that any food had been consumed since I'd left.

Things were dire. Jane and I just didn't know what to do for the best. Then two weeks later everything changed. My Mum fell on one of their walks and fractured her femur. Following hospital treatment, we arranged for her to be discharged to a superb care home, and Dad, who had temporarily been with Jane, joined her. Jane and I were so relieved that they were now somewhere safe and being cared for 24 hours a day.

They had a lovely double room with its own sitting area and a little patio. We took furniture and personal items in, including, at Dad's request, parking Walter, Dad's beloved bike, outside their French windows. They spent hours just sitting together on a sofa, holding hands. This is not to say that Jane did not at first get the daily phone calls from Dad demanding that they went back to their flat, but each time he accepted that Mum needed care and he would not leave her.

Dad then sadly had a stroke, and it became even more essential that they were being cared for in an appropriately equipped and staffed environment.

The staff fell over backwards to help my parents adjust to their new surroundings.

After dinner in the dining room, they would serve them coffee in the lounge. Mum and Dad, thinking they were on holiday in a hotel, used to then ask for the bill and were delighted when told,

"Dinner was a special free offer tonight."

The staff over time became our parents' only friends, as when Mum and Dad developed dementia their numerous friends seemed to abandon them. Excuses included not wanting to upset my parents if they did not recognise people. I actually think it was more about people protecting themselves from becoming upset, or for a few it was to avoid any expected regular commitment. What they did not seem to realise was how supportive Jane and I would have found it if they had visited.

Jane visited more than once a week and I came north to see them at least once a month. We rarely visited together as, when I could be around, I felt it only right to give Jane a break. The staff had got to know Jane well. They laughed at her instructions not to allow me to touch the jigsaws she sat working on during her visits. I have always hated jigsaws, and she reckoned it took her ages to remove the pieces I had wrongly hammered in.

Even after all my years in nursing roles, I found visiting extremely stressful. The home tried to provide some entertainment. I was delighted to join in Saturday Bingo! Dad hated Bingo and preferred a game of snakes and ladders. Mum was just happy looking through picture magazines. As Dad deteriorated music became our main shared pastime. We sang along vigorously to Nana Mouskouri, Gracie Fields, and Edith Piaf. Staff enthusiastically joined in.

It is difficult to admit that, although I loved them so much, it was always a relief when a visit was over. I will never forget sitting in the car crying after visits, when my father aggressively lashed out at me, and when I realised my mother had, for the first time, no idea who I was. I think she knew she liked me, but she was really happy to be hugged by anyone.

In December 2010 she peacefully passed away. I had only left her side ten minutes before but am always comforted by the fact that the Matron, who was wonderful, was with her at the end. Until the funeral I decided to return to work, which obviously to some seemed strange or even heartless, but I had lost my Mum, and done my crying, many years before her actual death.

We all worried about the impact Mum's death would have on my father. They were so in love until the very end and had never had a night apart in nearly 60 years. Dad's Alzheimer's had however progressed to such a point that he never really seemed to grasp she had gone. At Mum's funeral he merely commented on the blueness of the crematorium carpet, and asked me repeatedly, "What is in that box?"

Jane and I had decided that Dad should only come to the crematorium, and a male nurse kindly accompanied him and then took him straight back to the home. What we did not know from the nurse, or from the matron and other staff who came to the church service, was that, that day, visiting at the nursing home had been halted due to Norovirus. I was returning straight from the funeral lunch to London, but before leaving I just wanted to check Dad was OK.

Jane and I arrived at the home door with the flowers from the funeral bouquet. I was distraught when an officious new sister took the flowers and then refused us entry. We explained we had come from my Mum's funeral, that we would go straight to Dad in his room, touching nothing and seeing only him. She refused to budge, physically barring our entry. I lost it and started to pompously lecture her on nursing compassion and infection control, but then I glanced at Jane, who quietly pleaded with me to 'let it go'. The day had been traumatic enough. We left and I caught the train, still fuming about the unfeeling behaviour of a professional colleague. I can accept now that I probably overreacted as Dad would have been unaware of the reason for our visit.

I am sure my Dad missed my mother's presence. When we visited, he was often sitting holding another old lady's hand, and he apparently often called out Mum's name in the night. The staff learnt to distract him with chocolate!

As he became increasingly uncooperative and aggressive, chocolate bribery also played an important role in getting him washed and dressed. The nursing home staff handled him so well, with calm kindness and lots of singing. Even when he had lost the ability to speak, he still enjoyed singing. When we arrived at the home and were approaching his room, it was so comforting to hear staff and Dad singing along to familiar tunes.

By December 2012 Dad had deteriorated to such an extent that the matron suggested time had come to apply for NHS Continuing Healthcare Funding. Jane was hesitant as she had tried to seek funding for my Mum in the weeks before she died, and the application had been rejected. Although Mum was bed bound and required full nursing care, due to good care she did not meet the funding criteria; she did not have a pressure sore; her incontinence was well managed; she was not tube fed, and she was not aggressive. In a way we were relieved that she didn't meet these criteria.

Dad, because of his stroke and aggression, was in a very different position, and by 2012 my parents' money was running out. We decided to apply. An appointment was agreed for the January. I took a day off work and paid the £272 day return train fare to be present. Then it snowed. Jane and I arrived to be told that the meeting had just been cancelled because one of the panel said she couldn't make it the three miles from her home! I returned to London.

Then, in the February, to our surprise, and the astonishment of the Matron who had not been consulted, we received a letter saying the panel had met in our absence and the application had been rejected. We were furious and demanded that a properly constituted panel reconsidered Dad's application. The new meeting was eventually arranged for June. I went into civil service preparation mode, reading and making notes on all relevant documents and policies.

When we arrived, the Matron rushed to let us in and whispered that the nurses knew I was the Interim Chair of the NMC, the nursing regulator, and that my sister was a medical Consultant. She had overheard the senior nurse reviewer saying to the mental health nurse and social worker, "Remember, whoever they are and whatever they say we are not agreeing to this."

"We will see," was my calm response.

The meeting chaired by the senior nurse began with introductions. She held forth listing her various nursing qualifications, master's degree, and experience. The mental health nurse followed in a similar vein and I was next.

"I am Judith, and I am David's daughter," I said, followed by my sister who stated, "I am Jane, and I am David's other daughter."

The Matron and Social Worker simply gave their names and jobs.

We then went through criterion by criterion. It was an agonisingly slow process. The senior nurse became more and more defensive and aggressive as, point by point, we provided evidence that my father met the government policy stated level of care that justified funding. The mental health nurse looked grossly embarrassed, and the social worker amused. There was obviously no love lost between him and the senior nurse.

A particularly interesting moment was when the senior nurse was arguing that feeding was not an issue, in spite of the Matron describing how difficult it was to feed my father due to a poor swallowing and gag reflex. We were sitting in a screened off area and suddenly a nurse shouted for help on the other side of the screen. The matron jumped up, pulled the screen aside, and ran to help the nurse suction my Dad who was choking on his soup. No comment was made as she returned and calmly carried on with the meeting.

After two and a half hours the Senior Nurse announced, "We will consider what we have heard and will let you know our decision."

Very coolly and calmly I stated, "Thank you. We will wait to hear from you but can I just state, not as any sort of threat but as a fact, and to be totally open and honest, that if you do not agree that the criteria for funding have been met, we will be escalating this to the Clinical Commissioning Group, and, if need be, to the Region and Health Service Ombudsman."

Jane and I then left, with Jane very amused. She had never before seen me in my professional 'don't mess with me' mode. Dad's funding, backdated to February, was agreed a week before his death, in July 2013.

Dad sadly did not have an easy death, and his death had not been imminently expected. I still feel guilty that Jane had to handle it all without me as I was out of the country on NMC business. My phone rang just as I and my colleague, Ali, were in a British Embassy Car on our way to Putrajaya, to see the Malaysian Government Nurse, an imposing lady who I had found quite scary at a previous meeting. I burst into tears in the car, and Ali and the driver, flummoxed as to how to help, handed me tissues and water and offered to postpone the meeting. Having recovered from the initial shock I insisted we proceeded as it was night-time in the UK and, if we completed our meeting, I would be free to help Jane with calls once UK daytime arrived.

Ali and I were greeted at the Ministry with the usual formalities, and I thought I was coping well with a difficult conversation until Ali, realising I was struggling, gently announced,

"I am afraid Judith has just had some very sad news. Her father has just died in the UK."

The atmosphere immediately changed. I found myself engulfed in a hug from the usually distant Government Nurse. We were hurriedly reassured of her support in reviewing regulation of Nurses in the Insular Region and dispatched to pack and travel home.

Dad's funeral was family only. Dementia had claimed both my parents.

My sister and I joke when we cannot remember names or places, but behind that mirth lies a genuine concern for me that I will succumb to this cruel condition. I never want to be a burden to those I love. I have no fear of care in a nursing home, and just hope I can accept with good grace and good humour what lies ahead. I want to remember and ultimately be remembered for the incredible life I have led. Hence this book.

These memoirs end, a gift from me
To help you all quite clearly see
How new flight paths can be found,
Why hurdles that seem all around,
Should never stop a bird in flight
When new adventures are in sight.

THE END

ABOUT THE AUTHOR

Professor Judith Ellis OBE is a registered nurse who has had an extraordinary 42 year career.

Having trained as a Nightingale Nurse at St Thomas's Hospital London in the 1970s she initially pursued a clinical career in paediatric nursing but then went on to have many different health service related roles, including being: a University Lecturer; Senior Civil Servant; a Director at Great Ormond Street Children's Hospital, London; a University Pro Vice Chancellor/Executive Dean; a Council Member and the Interim Chair of the largest Healthcare Regulator in the world; and she ended her paid career as the Chief Executive of a Medical Royal College. Throughout her life she has undertaken health related charity activity and for over 20 years she has used any free time to volunteer in Low Income Countries. In retirement she continues to Chair a global health partnership charity. She has many qualifications, including a doctorate, is a member of many prestigious organisations, and as well as the Queen awarding her an MBE in 1998 and an OBE in 2019, she has received numerous nursing and health service related Awards.

Printed in Great Britain
by Amazon